The Talk About
The Chambers of Chenaniah

"Pastor John Coleman has written an impactful work for the modern day church! His insight into the heart of the worship leader will inspire songwriters, musicians, psalmists, and worshippers into a relentless pursuit of more than music. I strongly recommend this book and consider it a treasure that will bring greater insight into worship in the modern day church."
~ Trent Cory, International Worship Leader, Minister, Songwriter

"After reading this book, I am convinced that it is a must have for every pastor, every worship leader, and anyone who wants to experience true worship. John captures the very essence of the heart of this subject as he leads the reader through the three chambers. I am confident that once you have taken this journey you will conclude, as did I, that worship truly is an experience and not an event!"
~ Bishop Alvernis L. Johnson, Kingdom Life Ministries, Saginaw & Flint, MI

"*The Chambers of Chenaniah* is a gift to the Body. Pastor Coleman's gift of infusing spirituality with sensibility makes the entire concept of worship understandable and exciting. This practical, yet powerful, breakdown of the nuts and bolts of Who, why, and how we worship is an undeniable stepping stone, not only in the life of a worship leader, pastor, or minstrel but for every believer's relationship with our Father."
~ Senior Pastor Doug Taylor, Rebirth Christian Fellowship, Birmingham, AL

"As a music educator, somehow I thought that the trained musician was also a skillful musician. After reading this book,

I discovered that they are very different. John Coleman beautifully tells personal stories and brings to life the story of Chenaniah, "Master of the Song." Now I'm compelled to go deeper in worship; not while I'm on stage but in my everyday walk with the Lord. Experienced or novice, every worship leader, musician & singer should read this book!"
~ Alan Franklin, Co-Founder of MuzicNet School of Music, Dolton & Park Forest, IL

"This book causes us to graduate from religion to relationship! The truths in *The Chambers of Chenaniah* will pull the slack out of how we fellowship with God! If you desire increased sensitivity to the Holy Spirit, this is a must read. Every Christian singer and musician (even those who are not musically inclined) should read and learn from the truths found in this book."
~ Aaron Franklin, Co-Founder of MuzicNet School of Music, Dolton & Park Forest, IL

"The Davidic Anointing & the Chenaniah Calling are evident in Pastor John Coleman! Allow the Holy Spirit to give you revelation from His heart as you read *Chambers of Chenaniah!*"
~ Pastor Jon Jones, Worship & Arts Pastor, Christian Life Center, Tinley Park, IL and Atmosphere of Heaven Worship Group

"This book is a tool for every worshipper." St John 4:23–24: "Yet a time is coming and has now come when true worshippers will worship the Father in spirit and in truth," for they are the kind of worshippers the Father seeks. God is spirit, and His worshippers must worship in the spirit and in truth. "Now is the time for the Chambers of Chenaniah."
~ Pastor Eric L. Ashby Sr., Co-Founder of Intimate Moments Marriage Encounter & Senior Pastor of Charity Church KC, Blue Springs, MO

THE CHAMBERS OF CHENANIAH

12 Foundational Truths to Praise & Worship

The Chambers of Chenaniah
12 Foundational Truths to Praise & Worship
Published by KishKnows, Inc. "The Bright Idea Company"
www.kishknows.com
708.252.DOIT

Unless otherwise noted, all scripture references are from the
King James Version of the Bible.

Copyright © 2013 by John Deland Coleman

ISBN 978-0-9700561-5-3

Printed in the United States of America

Dedication

In Loving Memory of my brother Reginald A. Coleman aka "St. Nick"

and

In memory of Cynthia Heath

Acknowledgements

To Juanita Cotton, who saw something in me I didn't see in myself. You started me on this journey of singing for the Lord.

To Tom Bynum, who imparted in me the importance and significance of a worshipper. You also birthed something in me that I now know I was destined to become. The passion and heart I have developed over the years is because of the initial deposit that you made. I'll never forget one of the first times the Word of the Lord was released through you. I haven't looked back since! Thanks a million!

To Pastors Eric and Winnie Ashby, you both have proven time and time again to be a tremendous example to follow for many, and the heart of gold that you possess is priceless. The faith and great attitude that you have always displayed even in the midst of adversity is unprecedented. There are no two people that I know who deserve all of the favor and blessings that life can bring more than you two. You have always chosen to worship despite your circumstances. Continue to do what you do for God. Blessings!

To Bishop I.V. and Bridget Hilliard, I am honored to be a part of your fellowship and to glean from the wisdom, knowledge, and example of faith as a son.

To Generation N-Ter-N, I am so proud of you all and how far you've come. You may not know that as I am stretching you, I'm stretching myself as well. You all give me something else to look forward to every week we connect.

To my family, you all are awesome! Thanks for allowing me to have those long nights of peace and quiet and the long days of writing this book. To my wife, Kisia, who helped in the process of making this a success, THANK YOU. To my awesome, gifted, and talented teenage daughter, Kennedy, I am so glad to have you by my side working with me on the worship team. I am glad to have you as a part of Generation N-Ter-N.

To my fellow worship chamber leaders, Adrienne Bynum Terry, Kimberly Sherese Miller, and Curtis "Busta" Brown, I have had the pleasure of working with you in the past, and I'm looking forward to more moments in the spirit with you. You all have the oil on your lives, and I am excited about your future in God!

To all of those who believed and supported me, thanks from the bottom of my heart. Your prayers and financial support mean the world to me.

Finally, to Kingdom Church International, the church where worship is always in order! I love you all!

Contents

Preface

Thank you so much for taking the time and making the investment in this book that the Lord has laid upon my heart to release. It is with great humility that I introduce these 12 Foundational Truths that I have discovered during my life time that have proven to be imperative in the productivity and success of praise and worship in our local church body.

Of course, for some of us, we understand the number 12 represents order, and it is also the number for government. Therefore, I believe these 12 Truths will help set in place order and establish the governmental structure for ministries to build effective worship teams. It is my deepest heart's cry that the spirit of God in you begins to expand and explode to new realms and heights in the area of worship.

"Sing unto him a new song; play skillfully with a loud noise."
Psalm 33:3

"Chenaniah was a spiritual editor. A writer is only as good as their 'Spiritual Editor,' Chenaniah. Spiritual songs are mastered by staying in the editing room of God's presence. In the natural, a Producer will take a song for a matter of days and develop it, taking out some things and putting in others. However, Chenaniah not only has the ability to do the same thing, but he has the ability to edit on the spot by bringing forth the prophetic songs of the Lord."

~ Tom Bynum ~

From the book *Chenaniah, The Master of the Song*

CHENANIAH

Introduction

1 Chronicles 15:22: "And Chenaniah, chief of the Levites, was for song...because he was skillful."

Chenaniah's name is very rare in the Scriptures, yet he played a very significant role in the worship service. Chenaniah is found recorded in the Bible at least three times:

- 1 Chronicles 15:22 as referenced above
- 1 Chronicles 15:27 – "And David was clothed with a robe of fine linen, and all the Levites that bare the ark, and the singers, and Chenaniah the master of the song with the singers: David also had upon him an ephod of linen."
- 1 Chronicles 26:29 – "Of the Izharites, Chenaniah and his sons were for the outward business over Israel, for officers and judges."

Chenaniah's name here denotes "Yaweh Empowers," or "Established by God." Chenaniah was established and empowered by God as a master of the song that assisted in the carrying of the ark of the Lord. Those who operate as the leaders over our worship services must be able to assist with ushering in God's presence.

Chenaniah, along with David, is mentioned by name among those who carried the ark of the Lord from the house of Obededom. Although there were many great men and women of God in the Old Testament, out of all these great vessels of God, the Lord put a grace on Chenaniah to assist with carrying His presence.

Chenaniah was distinguished as "The Master of the Song," which set him apart from the other singers. When you read this chapter in its entirety, you will notice that everyone was given a task to do.

We can't all lead worship. We can't all play the keyboard or the drums. Everyone is allotted a specific grace to fulfill their purpose. Just imagine if everyone wanted to do the exact same thing in church! What a tremendous dilemma we would have on our hands not to mention the fact that we would not get anything accomplished. Paul even talks about how there are many different administrations of the gifts, but they're all of the same Spirit. (1 Corinthians 12:4)

The one gifted for worship is the one that should be operating in that office. Understand, though, that it is not all about performance and skill. A worship leader needs to have the grace as well. A grace on your gift would imply that the task at hand comes easier for you than others; it could also come naturally for you. Nevertheless, there is and has to be a skill that goes with the grace to lead in worship. We'll discuss this further later in the book.

Chenaniah, as the Master of the Song and one that was skilled, knew how to flow in the appropriate time. He was over thousands of minstrels and musicians. I believe the reason why so many ministries struggle in the area of having a minstrel (one who flows skillfully on the instrument) versus just a musician (one who has been trained to play the instrument) is because we emphasize being trained over being skillful. When a person is leading the worship service in song or on the instrument and is just trained and not skillful, it can prohibit healthy worship. I'll give more clarity to this later in the book.

Characteristics of Chenaniah

In order to be skillful as a worship leader, you must recognize the voice of God. This here is a very sensitive area in our churches because we have people that have been called to be worship leaders, but they are immature and not ready yet to walk in the call. These are sometimes the same people that we place in a position because they appear to be very gifted.

It is important to not have a worship arts ministry where someone is leading with a gifting alone. The truth is you need more than just your gifting.

The worship leader must have *character, sensitivity* to the Spirit, and *an intimate relationship* with the Lord.

In this area of worship, there has to be a man or woman who has been ordained of God. We have too many "spot fillers" in the church today. In other words, there are people that are in positions only because the positions need to be filled. As a result of this, quite a few of our worship services suffer. We have people getting up and singing the wrong songs. Others have somewhat of a flow, but then they get side-tracked and begin to drift completely in another direction. It is important for those of us who are of the Levite tribe to be ready to create an atmosphere conducive for the Word of God to be received.

As a part of this tribe, much responsibility falls on the minstrel, the psalmist,(I'll define these two more later), and the worship team. We need the Levites to really stand up for the Kingdom and be accounted for.

Spiritual Sensitivity

One reason for my taking a leap of faith in the creation of this book is because for some time now I have had a passion for God's people to know Him not only just through religious acts of service but to really know Him through relationship.

I strongly discerned that in this season of the church, we must be a people that have ears to hear what the Lord is saying. God is clearly speaking today through the sound of music and through yielded vessels. God has something to say in the earth today, and sometimes it just does not come through the ministry of the Word alone, but it is released through the ministry of song as well.

The greatest demand in our worship services today is not an eloquent voice, awesome rhythm patterns and beats, or even spectacular "runs" with amazing pitches, but the greatest demand is for "Spiritual Sensitivity."

Those that have an ear let them hear the sound and Word of the Lord for this generation.

There are so many spiritual dynamics for those of us who incorporate praise and worship into our services. I strongly feel that we must learn to adjust our spiritual lenses and get an open vision of praise and worship because it plays such a pivotal part in our worship services.

The message of the kingdom is still the same; however, the methods have changed. We as the church should want to be relevant! In secular society, music is changing all the time with the seasons of life. As the church, we must continue to develop the Kingdom sound in the Earth.

I need you to understand me on this because when it comes to change or transition, you do have to determine what is non-negotiable! Understand that the Word of God is not negotiable, and it must not be tampered with. However, when it comes to the sound in the House of the Lord, there is a transition that needs to take place.

Praise and worship is also a non-negotiable. There is no debate! It is mandatory! That's it, and it's settled! It does not matter what denomination you are in or not in the body of Christ, whether Apostolic, Pentecostal, Methodist, Lutheran, Full Gospel, Catholic, Baptist, and so forth; praise and worship must always play a part in our worship services as well as our personal relationships with God.

As worshippers of God, we must make this commitment:

We do believe in the Holy Ghost!

We will not water the Word of the Lord down!

We will not dishonor His presence!

We believe in the power and importance of Praise and Worship, therefore we will not allow it to be diluted by traditions or the spirit of religion!

Let's make the decision right now, this very moment, to stay on the cutting edge of what God is doing in the Earth through music.

<u>Your Ear to God</u>

1 Samuel 3:1–10, 19:

"And the child Samuel ministered unto the LORD before Eli. And the word of the LORD was precious in those days; there was no open vision. And it came to pass at that time, when Eli was laid down in his place, and his eyes began to wax dim, that he could not see; And ere the lamp of God went out in the temple of the LORD, where the ark of God was, and Samuel was laid down to sleep; That the LORD called Samuel: and he answered, here am I. And he ran unto Eli, and said, Here am I; for thou calledst me. And he said, I called not; lie down again. And he went and lay down. And the LORD called yet again, Samuel. And Samuel arose and went to Eli, and said, Here am I; for thou didst call me. And he answered, I called not, my son; lie down again. Now Samuel did not yet know the LORD, neither was the word of the LORD yet revealed unto him. And the LORD called Samuel again the third time. And he arose and went to Eli, and said, here am I; for thou didst call me. And Eli perceived that the LORD had called the child. Therefore Eli said unto

Samuel, Go, lie down: and it shall be, if he call thee, that thou shalt say, Speak, LORD; for thy servant heareth. So Samuel went and lay down in his place. And the LORD came, and stood, and called as at other times, Samuel, Samuel. Then Samuel answered, Speak; for thy servant heareth. And Samuel grew, and the LORD was with him, and did let none of his words fall to the ground."

There will come a season when those who will lead God's people must learn how to hear the voice of the Lord. Scripture illustrates here in the story of the Prophet Samuel that he went through a season of discerning the Lord's voice. As a worship leader, before you get to a place of recognition, you must be in a place of sensitivity to God's voice.

Samuel grew in his intimacy and ability to hear God's voice so much so that the Bible says none of his words fell to the ground (1 Samuel 3:19). I believe, as a worship leader, you can arrive at such a place where you are so skilled and so sensitive to the spirit of the Lord that every time you step up to lead worship, none of the words you sing fall to the ground and God's presence comes in mightily. Glory to God!

But you have to go through the process of being proven!

In this story, Samuel was young, and at first he did not recognize what was unfamiliar to him, which was the Lord's voice. This is the same when it comes to flowing in worship. Immaturity can keep you from hearing what direction the worship needs to go in. You must be familiar with God's voice so that you know how to move when He says move and stop when He says stop.

If you're not in tune and skilled in hearing His voice, your gift without revelation will lead to devastation

&

your level of revelation will not exceed your level of worship!

What am I saying? The more you spend time in God's presence worshipping Him, your potential of revelation increases tremendously.

The Master of the Song

When you carry an anointing as the "Master of the Song," it is like being the Pied Piper, and you can lead a generation of people into the presence of the Lord. It is ironic to me how often Chenaniah's name is not discussed in our worship services, yet praise and worship plays such a vital role in them. There must be an emphasis and an implementation of the anointing of Chenaniah back into our houses of worship!

I believe that there are secular artists who have become Masters of the Song in their particular genre. They are operating in a Chenaniah-like anointing because they are very skilled and familiar with their craft. As a result, masses of people are following them. They are influencing nations and changing cultures.

I don't have to mention any of them here, but all you have to do is turn on the television, tune into the radio, look at a billboard, or even just go to your local restaurant and you will hear and even see the influence they have. Their music carries a force that is drawing this generation into their presence. Many of them are musicians and singers to the world, but to God, they were meant to be our modern day psalmists and minstrels.

I believe that not only is God calling the Church to wake up and begin to see this, but we must intercede for these artists. It's my desire and prayer that one of these days during an awards ceremony, the conviction of the Holy Spirit will come in and many of these people will really give their lives to Christ.

"I declare that a shift is coming in our music industry that's going to revolutionize it! I prophesy a Mantle Switch, a changing of the guards!

May the anointing of the Lord invade the hearts and minds of those who know Him and those who don't know Him, in Jesus' Name! There are so many sounds in the Earth today. But I declare that this anointing of Chenaniah will rise and awake a generation. May it arise from a slumber and sedated state!"

"And David spake to the chief of the Levites to appoint their brethren to be the singers with instruments of musick, psalteries and harps and cymbals, sounding, by lifting up the voice with joy." 1 Chronicles 15:16

Chamber One

True Worship Is Your First Connection to God

"The true, the genuine, worship is when man, through his spirit, attains to friendship and intimacy with God. True and genuine worship is not to come to a certain place; it is not to go through a certain ritual or liturgy; it is not even to bring certain gifts. True worship is when the spirit, the immortal and invisible part of man, speaks to and meets with God, who is immortal and invisible."

~ William Barclay ~

What is real worship? Is it something we do as believers on Sundays, special holidays, or in our mid-week service? Or does it involve surrendering ourselves to Him and presenting our lives unto Him? This question of real worship needs to be answered and understood throughout our Christian organizations. I believe worship should be that unwavering, unhindered connection that you have with your Creator because of who He is.

Webster's Dictionary defines worship as follows:

"from the Old English w*eorthscipe*; *weorth* meaning worthy + *scipe* meaning ship. Hence, a worthy ship, something or someone of worth or importance."

One of the most simplistic acts of worship is "giving due worth to God."

Worship in the Hebrew is *shachah*. It means "to prostate in homage or worship." This word can be found in the following scriptures: Psalm 95:6, Psalm 99:5, 1 Chronicles 16:29, and Psalm 22:27.

"O come, let us worship and bow down: let us kneel before the LORD our maker." Psalm 95:6

"Exalt ye the LORD our God, and worship at his footstool; for he is holy." Psalm 99:5

"Give unto the LORD the glory due unto his name: bring an offering, and come before him: worship the LORD in the beauty of holiness." 1 Chronicles 16:29

"All the ends of the world shall remember and turn unto the LORD: and all the kindreds of the nations shall worship before thee." Psalm 22:27

Worship in the Greek is *proskuneo*. "It means to prostate oneself in worship; to reverence, to adore; to kiss like a dog licking his master's hand." This word can be found in the following scriptures: Luke 4:8, Revelations 15:4, and John 4:22.

"And Jesus answered and said unto him, Get thee behind me, Satan: for it is written, Thou shalt worship the Lord thy God, and him only shalt thou serve." Luke 4:8

"Who shall not fear thee, O Lord, and glorify thy name? for thou only art holy: for all nations shall come and worship before thee; for thy judgments are made manifest." Revelations 15:4

"Ye worship ye know not what: we know what we worship: for salvation is of the Jews." John 4:22

The Greek word *proskuneo* for kiss meaning to show affection implies that you can't worship God without showing affection. Worship demands that we demonstrate our feelings for God. If we are ever going to plan on seeing the supernatural in our lives, our connection to God through worship must be in order.

My connection that I have with God speaks more volumes than any expression or form of worship I could give apart from Him.

Theopedia.com/worship explains worship as follows:

> "Worship is an active response to the character, words and actions of God, initiated by His revelation and enabled by His redemption, whereby the mind is transformed (e.g. belief, repentance), the heart is renewed (e.g. love, trust), and actions are surrendered (e.g. obedience, service), all in accordance with His will and in order to declare His infinite worthiness.

> In both Hebrew and Greek, there are two categories of words for worship. The first is about body language that demonstrates respect and submission; to bow down, to kneel, to prostrate oneself.

> The second is about doing something for God that demonstrates sacrifice and obedience; to offer, to serve.

~ 15 ~

Worship is the submission of all our nature to God. It is the quickening of conscience by His holiness; the nourishment of mind with His truth; the purifying of imagination by His Beauty; the opening of the heart to His love; the surrender of will to His purpose and all of this gathered up in adoration, the most selfless emotion of which our nature is capable and therefore the chief remedy for that self-centeredness which is our original sin and the source of all actual sin."

This is a word for someone specific right now: God says if you really get connected to Me above all else and everything else, I will put you on My VIP list! Glory to God! God says I will surprise you. Get ready to reap in places you haven't sown, and I'll give you access, clearance to favor unheard of. I'm the God of Abraham, Isaac, and Jacob. I'll give you things that you didn't have to ask for, because I am God. I am that I am says the Lord.

You must stay in faith. Even though God is all powerful, omnipotent, omnipresent, and all knowing, there is one thing that God Himself cannot do and that is worship Himself. This is one of the reasons He created us!

Calling All Worshippers!

So He seeks those who will worship Him in spirit and in truth. The word *truth* implies sincerity of the heart. So in essence here, I don't worship God because I have a need. I worship God because He has need of my worship! We were made for His good will and pleasure. When I worship, I give God pleasure.

"And as they went to tell his disciples, behold, Jesus met them, saying, 'Rejoice!' So they came and held him by the feet and worshiped him." Matthew 28:9 (NKJV)

"God is Spirit, and those who worship him must worship in spirit and truth." John 4:24 (NKJV)

"Then the four living creatures said, 'Amen!' And the twenty-four elders fell down and worshiped him who lives forever and ever." Revelation 5:14 (NKJV)

Now let me just jump right in here and state for the record that I know I may offend some people or make them upset when I say what I have to say. I need you to understand the heart of God here. Worship is not music, and worship is not songs; it is not the organ or the keyboard or even the worship team singing. The songs, the singing, the dancing, the hip hop rap culture, and even drama are all expressions of worship. Giving and serving in your local church is an expression of worship.

For so long in our churches, we have identified songs and music as worship. However, the fact of the matter is we can't limit worship to a box form. God is so much bigger than what we can imagine. We have yet to even scratch the surface of God. In the most simplistic form, "Worship is our first connection to God."

The reality is that being connected to Jesus is everything. When you're in love with Jesus, you have to fight sometimes to stay connected. It's like when you're in love with that special someone; you think about them all the time. You can't imagine your life without them. This is how our love should be for Jesus. We often sing songs like, "I'm in love with Jesus and He's in love with me." However, do we really know what we are saying at times? Sometimes we sing songs because they sound good.

Offense Disconnects You

One thing I have discovered about worship is that when you have offense and resentment in your heart, it's so much harder to press into worship. Offense can become a stumbling block keeping the presence of God from invading your heart and life. We all at some point or another have struggles with offenses in certain areas of life. The truth of the matter is life happens, situations happen, people walk in and out of your life, and people pass on. When this is the case, we have to learn to play with the hand that has been dealt to us.

People get offended just from attending church sometimes. If God does not move the way you want Him to move; or if they aren't singing the kind of songs you like; or the minister is not preaching what you want to hear; you get offended. You can allow this to cause barriers, and if you are not careful, it will "make you barren."

There's nothing like being in a relationship with Jesus. You can't afford to allow offense and other things to disconnect you from His presence. As Kim Walker-Smith of *Jesus Culture* said:

"One day you will live in the fruit of your moment."

So you cannot afford to miss your moments with God due to offense. It's very important that your heart is always connected to Jesus.

"Keep thy heart with all diligence; for out of it are the issues of life." Proverbs 4:23

If the enemy can infiltrate your mind and heart, he'll have a stronghold over you. There are so many things that can affect your heart: things of the world, people and situations, the loss of a love one, a job, a house, or an automobile. The enemy knows how much your heart is tied to your material possessions. So he'll come in to get you off track and cause you to lose focus and, ultimately, sight of Jesus.

As John 4:23 says, "It's time, as worshipers of God, to give Him all we have. For when he is exalted, everything about me is decreased. So many times we stand in the way of really stepping into the secret place of worship with God. Just abandon tradition and the 'expected' ways of Praise & Worship and get lost in the holy of holies with the sole intention of blessing the Father's heart." ~ Jessica Leah Springer ~

Doorkeepers to Worship

For those that are worship leaders, the important thing to remember in serving God's people in the expression of praise and worship is that you must be like a doorman and a door keeper. You have to present yourself and represent the character of God as you stand on your post to lead His people to the place of worship.

Sundee Frazier explains the concept of doorkeepers in "The Importance of Being a Worship Leader" as follows:

> "Being a doorkeeper (a worship leader) is a significant position because worship opens people to God. There may be people in the service that you're leading that may have never really encountered God. Some of them may just be in a rough place in life. However, because of your relationship with God, you lead them to this place where they too can connect with Him and something happens that causes hope to be activated in them again. You have introduced them to the true and living God.
>
> It emboldens us to believe the truth that God really is as good as, and loves us as much as, we'd hoped. In this place of belief, we are able to put our trust back in God. We see reality (about ourselves, others and the world) through God's eyes, and we more eagerly desire to be aligned with God's heart, will and purposes.
>
> Of course this doesn't happen fully for every person each time we gather to worship God. And to what degree it happens for someone is not dependent on us. However, worship has the potential to bring people before God, and worship leaders assist by standing at the door and welcoming them in.
>
> On the flip side, if worship leaders don't take their positions seriously, they can block the doorway, making it more difficult for worshipers to enter God's

presence."
(http://cms.intervarsity.org/slj/article/2436/0.1)

"Worship has the potential to bring people before God, and worship leaders assist by standing at the door and welcoming them in."

~ Sundee Frazier ~

Worship Reconnects

In life in general, we experience the ups and downs. We have kids and jobs and other things that go on during the week that at times can cause us to feel or get disconnected from God. So people come to church and are looking for assistance to be reconnected again. The connection that we have to God is and should be the most important thing in our lives.

Keeping an Open Spirit to God

We need to be open to how He wants to move in our lives in order to reconnect. We often fail in our churches when we look for God to move on a certain song. The truth is, if your heart is ready to receive, then so will it be unto you. It's just like when someone begins to tarry for the Holy Spirit; some receive and some don't. They are not open enough to God. They have it in their head but not in their heart.

"Always learning and never able to arrive at a knowledge of the truth." 2 Timothy 3:7 (ESV)

Everyone's faith and hunger level are not the same. I've witnessed people coming into the house of God, and before the worship service really kicks in gear, they are already gone somewhere in worship. I love to see people come in and they are "wired" like that. There's no pumping or priming the pump because they are ready for a move of God.

These types of worshippers really motivate me in my leading worship and writing music. Just to see the expressions that come from them as they press in to the presence of God is priceless. My heart longs and aches to see His people connecting with Him not just when we're together but taking that experience home as they continue to worship. Worship for these kinds of people is more than just songs.

Real Worship

What happens if no songs are sung? Will you still worship? I love the song by Wess Morgan that says, "I choose to worship."

I mean if no one will, I will. I choose to worship.

Real worship is the lifestyle that I now live because of my connection to Him. Some of us have a testimony, as the old church mothers would say, "If it had not been for the Lord who was on my side, I don't know where I would be."

I remember years ago when I first gave my life to the Lord and I didn't know what to expect. I just knew Jesus saved me and that I wasn't going to hell when I died. I had not had the best life as a child. However, I've learned to make lemonade out of lemons. Growing up in a neighborhood full of gangs and poverty, drugs and prostitution, there was always something going down in our area. As the years went by and I began to grow in the things of God, something was stirring inside me. I didn't understand, but God was igniting a fire in me for worship.

"Without worship, we go about miserable."

~ A. W. Tozer ~

God Connects with Us in Our Youth

Some time ago I recall one night I had a dream and I saw myself standing in the hallway of our old apartment. The living room was so dark, and as I was standing in the hallway, I felt a strong force pulling on my body. I was wondering what was going on. Then I remember the force getting stronger and stronger. In the dream, I was just a child, and I was scared. Then I started seeing what appeared to be dark images moving around that had unusual shapes to them. I started crying, but no one heard me.

Next, out of nowhere, a light appeared behind from my kitchen, and I heard a voice saying, "You don't have to go. You don't have to go." God was assuring me that if no one else protected me, He would. God had been dealing with me, but I just didn't understand the calling then.

This dream was very clear in the sense I literally felt like death was trying to assassinate me. Ever since I was a child, I can remember having dream after dream. However, this one in particular was one I'll never forget.

As I began to put these dreams into perspective, I realized that as a young person, I had developed a heart and ear for music. Often, I'd be sitting in the house with my mom or in my room listening to music. Little did I know that the hand of God was on my life and He wanted to use my love for music for His glory. From that dream, I have learned that the forces of darkness will always try to pull on you to surrender to their way.

When I was a young adult, I had singing groups and musicians that tried to persuade and entice me to sing with them and for the world. I remember being so enticed by the devil to the point where he literally tried to get me to use my gift for the world. I praise God for revelation back then and ordering my steps so much so that I am now walking in my assignment. Years ago I didn't understand those dreams, but, boy, do I get them now!

Jesus had been covering me all my life. From the hit and run incident when I was a child, to the guns and knives held up to me; from being suicidal during a difficult time in my life. Jesus had been connecting with me, but I didn't even know it. Man, I'm so glad He didn't give up on me!

My worship is for real!

I have been there in my life where I know some people may even be right now: loving God and loving the world. I did that thing as religious Christians do on Sundays too. I went to church, but I still did my own thing. I was propositioned several times to go secular. But God had such a call on my life. I just didn't know it.

I remember one day I finally made up my mind to worship God with all of my heart. Because of that, He has opened doors in my life, and my love for Him has ever increased. I got a revelation of praise and worship, and the rest is history. You may be struggling with your calling, but I'm telling you, as a witness, God is so faithful.

When you put your trust in Him, He will never disappoint you. Even when you can't trace Him at times, you must still trust Him. Because of my constant connection to God and staying in His face, it literally saved my life.

"Seek the LORD, and his strength: seek his face evermore." Psalm 105:4

"Turn us again, O LORD God of hosts, cause thy face to shine; and we shall be saved." Psalm 80:19

The Greek word for face here, *enopion,* means in the face of, before, in the presence (sight) of.

Right now maybe you're beginning to reflect on all of what God's done in your life too. I release you right now to just worship. God is so faithful. Seek His face.

The Spiritual Connection

Again Sundee Frazier brings up a very important point regarding our connection with God in an article entitled "Connecting with God…and Not Just Singing Songs":

> "True worship from a person to God requires a spiritual connection that worship leaders can't force,

control or manipulate. We have to trust God and God's work in people. This trust requires us to get into place as doorkeepers in the house party of God. (Psalm 84:10) And, along with God, welcome fellow worshipers in to participate. We cannot make worship happen, but with thoughtfulness, persistence and a willingness to take risks we can get people into the house and then help them have the courage to approach the throne. Once there, they can thank Him for the great things he has done for them or have that heart-to-heart talk they've been needing to have." (http://cms.intervarsity.org/slj/article/1465)

As a church, we are forever learning new things. In the place of worship, we often fall short because we tend to make it about the new thing and not Him. I love the song by Israel Houghton, "Jesus at the Center of It All." We must keep it about Him.

This is how our churches should function, with Jesus being the center. Not us, not the pastor, the praise team, the minstrels, the "new things," but Jesus! I believe we will see God in such a way we've never witnessed Him before.

I've been to many worship conferences and church events, and it never ceases to amaze me how we can get so caught up in the mechanics of ministry and not the power of His presence. If you want your worship experiences not to be hindered or limited, you must stay connected to the Source. When anything that requires power is disconnected from its source, it fails to perform its original purpose. As my Bishop says,

"Stay focused, stay in faith, and most importantly, stay connected."

~ Bishop I.V. Hilliard ~

True Worship Requires Passion & Pursuit

"When it comes to worship, I have to believe the entire song that I am singing. I can't just sing words. I have to believe what I'm saying; I have to fill it in my heart. I have to be able to put my passion in what is coming out of me."

~ Kim Walker-Smith ~

"God is a Spirit: and they that worship him must worship him in spirit and in truth." John 4:24

Passion is simply defined as "an intense emotion." Passion is what drives you when you can't see the way. Passion is the fire that purifies and validates your love and affection towards one person or a thing. Passion is that thing that keeps you moving when others give up and throw in the towel. From personal experience, I have found out that in life, most people that say they are passionate about something really aren't. Dr. Miles Monroe said:

"The proof of passion is in the pursuit!"

What are you passionate about the most in life? Is it family, friends, your job, business, or other material things? Believe it or not, whatever you think about the most reveals the real you. When it comes to worshipping your Creator, your Lord, Abba God, the King of kings, the Lord of lords, do you go all out?

When given the opportunity to praise and worship Him, do you take full advantage of the moment? You can never duplicate a moment in the raw presence of God. So don't miss your moment in worship!

"Never let a single moment in time affect who you are as a worshipper."

~ Tom Bynum ~

I can recall on several occasions in my early years of salvation when it came time for praise and worship in the church, I just didn't know what to expect. I was inexperienced in this area. The whole concept of praise and worship was foreign to me, but there was always something down inside of me longing for more. I found out later that it was more of God that I wanted.

I'm quite sure you can identify and relate to this to some extent, whether you have been in a dry, dead church or in a place of spiritual drought, or perhaps the church you attend has no revelation of praise and worship. I just want to declare unto you that the moisture of heaven and the oil of His glory are available. God has always been omnipresent. We have just shut the door to letting Him in all areas of our personal lives.

I remember in the early years of my walk with God, I'd be sitting in church in what we used to call testimony service. I can remember it like it was yesterday. I felt like I wanted more. Although I was participating in the choirs and musicals, that was not enough. Back then, those groups were as close as I got to praise and worship. But then there were times I'd be sitting in service and I'd hear music in my head, but it wasn't the typical A and B selections. I did not know it, but even back then I was longing for more.

God so desires to be intimate with us. James 4:8 tells us as we draw near to God, He will draw near to us. Understand this, child of God:

> **It takes more than just God coming to you!**
> **You have to know how to go to Him!**

The Pursuit

Now let's look at this word *pursuit*. *Pursuit* denotes: to chase, to hunt after, to aspire or to strive for (Webster's Dictionary). In other words, you must push forward and press through offense, oppression, attack, distractions, disappointments, defeat, and fear, just to name a few.

The enemy would love to have you become disoriented and confused when it comes to praise and worship. However, this is where you must persevere. Begin eliminating things and people that may try to distract, prevent, and block you from getting to God. You must be determined and have a mind and heart fixed on Him. You must have your face set like a flint! (Isaiah 50:7)

Let's use King David as our example. He was a man that was no stranger to the posture, position, and place of worship. In Psalm 16:11, David talks about being in the raw presence of God, where there is the fullness of joy—the indescribable, undeniable presence of God.

1 Samuel 30:1–8:

> "On the third day David and his men came to Ziklag.
> Now the Amalekites had raided the Negev and
> Ziklag. They attacked Ziklag and burned it. They took
> captive the women who were in it, from the youngest
> to the oldest, but they did not kill anyone. They
> simply carried them off and went on their way. When
> David and his men came to the city, they found it
> burned. Their wives, sons, and daughters had been
> taken captive. Then David and the men who were
> with him wept loudly until they could weep no more.
> David's two wives had been taken captive – Ahinoam
> the Jezreelite and Abigail the Carmelite, Nabal's
> widow. David was very upset, for the men were
> thinking of stoning him; each man grieved bitterly
> over his sons and daughters.   But David drew
> strength from the Lord his God. Then David said to
> the priest Abiathar son of Ahimelech, 'Bring me the
> ephod.' So Abiathar brought the ephod to David.
> David inquired of the Lord, saying, 'Should I pursue
> this raiding band? Will I overtake them?' He said to
> him, 'Pursue, for you will certainly overtake them and
> carry out a rescue!'" (NET)

Notice that when you access the authentic presence of God,
it will encourage your heart and put a pursuit down on the
inside of you to be and do everything God has called you to.
It is my prayer and desire that a fire like never before for God
is ignited from within you and that the course of your life
shifts as a result of "True Worship."

We've been such a people that are accustomed to limited and even incorrect aspects, interpretations, and perspectives on worship. And unfortunately, the potential to become misinformed is more prevalent now. This is because many people have come from a place of *religion* and not *relationship*. As a result, we have gotten off track. But we must ask the question, "What does God really have to say about our worship?" Selah.

"The whole person, with all his senses, with both mind and body, needs to be involved in genuine worship."

~ Jerry Kerns ~

What Is True Worship?

Romans 12:1–2 (NIV) outlines what true worship is:

"Therefore, I urge you, brothers and sisters, in view of God's mercy, to offer your bodies as a living sacrifice, holy and pleasing to God—this is **your true and proper worship**. Do not conform to the pattern of this world, but be transformed by the renewing of your mind. Then you will be able to test and approve what God's will is—his good, pleasing and perfect will."

To better understand the question of what God thinks about our worship, we must answer some questions based off of the above scripture in Romans 12.

The Why of Worship

When we really take the time to reflect, we are reminded of God's mercies. Therefore, we worship the Lord because of His goodness, grace, and mercy shown toward us.

It is in Him that we live, move and have our being (Acts 17:28 KJV).

Without Him we can do NO THING (John 15:5 KJV)!

We cannot breathe on our own, wake up on our own, and make it in life on our own. It is all because of God's grace! Everything that has been made available for us in life and eternity is because of God's grace provided for us through the precious blood of Jesus. A full understanding of this compels us to give Him true worship! It is the reason WHY WE WORSHIP!

The How of Our Worship

The "how of our worship" involves us presenting our bodies to God as a *living sacrifice*. We understand that in our flesh dwells no good thing (Romans 7:18). However, we can cause our flesh to be subject to the will of God through the process of renewing our minds. We can only renew our minds by accepting and acting on the truth of God's Word.

As we submit our minds, wills, emotions, imaginations, and intellects (the soul-ish part of us) to this process, it becomes easier for our bodies to do what they should do. Our hands will lift up in surrender, our feet will be free to move, and our legs will want to stand or bow in worship. We will be able to press past fatigue, sickness, frustration, and heaviness. This is all possible because we have an understanding of the why of worship, and now we are embracing the how.

"No man gives anything acceptable to God until he has first given himself in love and sacrifice."

~ A.W. Tozer ~

The renewing of the mind goes hand and hand with the sanctification process. We can be living sacrifices only if we have submitted to the sanctification process. The sanctification process requires submission to the authority of God's Word (John 17:17). This truth liberates us to give true worship—our entire being.

"And ye shall know the truth, and the truth shall make you free." John 8:32

It is the conviction that truth brings followed by your internal and external actions of worship that is true worship.

Music is just an external motivator that influences our minds, wills, emotions, imaginations, intellects, and eventually our bodies to participate. It is a compelling tool that we can use to assist in our expression of worship to God.

If we worship God aside from being true, we are hypocrites, and He sees right through our hypocrisy. Look at God's response to those who worshipped in hypocrisy:

"I hate, I despise your feast days, and I will not smell in your solemn assemblies. Though ye offer me burnt offerings and your meat offerings, I will not accept them: neither will I regard the peace offerings of your fat beasts. Take thou away from me the noise of thy songs; for I will not hear the melody of thy viols. But let judgment run down as waters, and righteousness as a mighty stream." Amos 5:21–24

The Where & the What of Worship

True worship is centered totally around God. The "where" and the "what" of how we worship is not as important. Although it is very important to assemble with other believers to worship; although it is very important to have a hallowed out place for God; although it is very important to be in a certain atmosphere; the "external" where of worship is not as important as the "internal" where of worship. Jesus tells us that true worshipers will worship God in spirit and in truth (John 4:24).

It is important to not allow yourself to get too caught up in what music you should sing in worship, what you should wear, and what others think about it. Please understand, there should be definite guidelines, but focusing on these things more than the attitude of the heart should be avoided.

Additionally, although worship is a very personal and intimate engagement with God, it is very appropriate, acceptable, and biblical to do it in a public setting.

Psalm 22:22 – "I will declare thy name unto my brethren: in the midst of the congregation will I praise thee."

Psalm 35:18 – "I will give thee thanks in the great congregation: I will praise thee among much people."

The Who of Worship

It's also important to realize that worship is reserved only for God. "Then saith Jesus unto him, Get thee hence, Satan: for it is written, Thou shalt **worship** the Lord thy God, and him **only** shalt thou serve." Matthew 4:10

We are not to worship ministry gifts, such as pastors, apostles, prophets, saints, famous people, entertainers, statues, angels, any false gods, etc., or Mary, the mother of Jesus. We also should not be worshipping for the expectation of something in return, such as a miraculous healing. Worship is done for God because He deserves it, and it is for His pleasure alone.

"The process of true worship is not based on a personality but on our passion which drives us straight to purpose."

~ John D. Coleman ~

TRUTH #3

True Worship Manifests God's Presence

"When God's people begin to praise and worship Him using the Biblical methods He gives, the Power of His presence comes among His people in an even greater measure."

~ Graham Truscott ~

True worship involves habitation, revelation, and manifestation of God's glory.

According to Dictionary.com, the word *habitation* means a place of residence, dwelling, or an abode. In other words, there's a point in praise and worship when God comes down in the midst of your problems and situations, and He hangs out with you until they go away. What a mighty God we serve!

David says in Psalm 22:3 – "But thou art holy, O thou that inhabitest the praises of Israel."

Bishop I.V. Hilliard's *Wisdom Insight* book defines *revelation* as:

> "The highest order of knowledge and understanding of the plan of God at my level of comprehension for which I am now accountable for. It is the product of the Holy Spirit breathing on the word of God and making it come alive in me. It is the ability to know beyond what you know, but you know that you know."

Now according to Merriam Webster's Dictionary, *revelation* is "the act of communicating divine truth; an act of revealing to view and to make known."

God is literally looking for sons and daughters to create an environment for Him to lodge in, not just on Sundays alone, but every day of the week. When a person learns this principle of inviting Him in through worship and praise, it becomes a lifestyle. When there's a revelation of praise and worship, you won't have to keep teaching it. I often say this to our own church:

A church's revelation will not exceed its level of worship.
Little worship equates to little revelation.
Heavy worship equates to heavy revelation.

"I consider that our present sufferings are not worth comparing with the glory that will be revealed in us. For the creation waits in eager expectation for the children of God to be revealed. For the creation was subjected to frustration, not by its own choice, but by the will of the one who subjected it, in hope that the creation itself will be liberated from its bondage to decay and brought into the freedom and glory of the children of God." Romans 8:18–21 (NIV)

Paul is saying here that there is a glory that God wants to reveal through you in the Earth. There is a nation, a people, a culture, a generation waiting for you to come out of the box, out of the ordinary, and out of the norm.

Earth's turmoil is an opportunity for God to be revealed through the true worshippers in the Earth. The real sons and daughters won't stop when others do. They will continue to press on.

> "The revelation of God is the fuel for the fire of our worship." ~ Matt Redman ~

The Environment of True Worship

Remember the story of Adam? God created Adam and put him in the garden and in charge of it. In the garden, there was an atmosphere of God's presence. Adam had everything in His presence. God was there with him. God walked with Adam because there was a relationship with Him. There was no need for religion. Religion is an attempt to get back "there" with God. Adam and God were already "there." The "there" is God's presence. As people of God, we must become lovers of His presence.

It also is interesting to note that God didn't create an environment where Adam had to find His presence, but instead, He put him in it. The presence of the Lord is where man belongs. God is our refuge! Often in life, whatever you are exposed to first becomes a part of your core, the real you. Unfortunately, Adam messed up and made the decision to trade God's presence for what he thought was missing out of his life—power.

It's important to notice also that Adam was placed in the Garden of Eden. According to *Strong's Exhaustive Concordance,* Eden was the region of Adam's home, and it comes from the Hebrew word *aednah* (feminine); it is from *adan* {ed-naw'}, which means: delicate, delight, pleasure. Today we cannot locate Eden on a physical map. Eden was an atmosphere.

Whether it was literal or not is not really the point. It was an atmosphere, a state of being. God placed Adam in an environment of pleasure. Sometimes as believers we can make the mistake of looking for God in a certain place.

God is not, cannot, and will not be limited to a place!

There's a place where I believe God intends for us as believers to never stray away from, and that is His presence.

The word *Eden* in the Hebrew context means "delightful, adornment, paradise, and pleasure; a state of perfect happiness or bliss or contentment." This was God's original intent for us. God created us in His image and likeness to worship Him and experience paradise while doing so.

<u>What Is Glory?</u>

I have done a bit of research [Adapted from http://www.dabhand.org. (*The Word Glory*)] on this and believe that it is important to include some of it here:

> "If you were to ask the average church member what the word *glory* means chances are they will give a vague or evasive answer. This is largely due to the limited definition of the word in English. The word *glory* in biblical context is translated in twenty different word forms; twelve in the Hebrew and eight in the Greek.
>
> There are 371 verses in which *glory* occurs in the Bible with 148 of them being a rendering of the word

ka^bo^d or ka^bad (masculine) which means *to be heavy*.

The first use is given in Gen 31:1 where it is used to describe the riches acquired by Jacob. *Glory* is also commonly rendered as *honor*.

A word rendered *glory* on one occasion is pa^'ar meaning beautify; to adorn or embellish.

Perhaps a word that most closely encapsulates the English perception of splendor is ha^da^r. It is derived from a root meaning to swell up and really means magnificence, ornamentation or splendor. The word is broadly rendered as glory, majesty, honor, beauty, comeliness, excellency, beauties, glorious and goodly.

A much more specific concept of glory is given on the one occasion *addereth* is rendered *glory*. The implication is that it is a cloak or mantel of glory rather than something inherent in the object itself. In fact the word is more generally rendered mantle, garment, goodly or robe.

A different concept of glory is given by the Hebrew word ha^lal which literally means *shine* and thus *to praise* or *to boast*. It is usually translated *praise* but on sixteen occasions it is rendered as *glory* in the sense of *glory* in His Holy Name.

Continuing the theme of praise sha^bach, which properly means to address in a loud tone, is also rendered glory on one occasion:

1 Chronicles 16:35 – "And say ye, Save us, O God of our salvation, and gather us together, and deliver us from the heathen, that we may give thanks to thy holy name, [and] **glory** in thy praise."

Again the word is more commonly rendered praise.

Another word rendered glory; to^har literally means brightness. It is similar to the shine meaning of ha^lal except the emphasis is not upon the outward effect of the brilliance so much as its inner character. The word is rare; rendered purifying and clear... The Aramaic word is also rendered as *honor* twice.

We therefore see that in the Old Testament the concept of glory really falls into three main areas.

Firstly, at least in terms of volume, is the sheer notion of weight. This is then extended into the concept of presence whether it is through ornamentation, 'swelling', cloaking or sheer inherent magnificence. Finally we see the notion of praise, praiseworthiness, shining or brilliance described as glory.

It is interesting that whilst the principle basis of glory in the Hebrew is the weight or immensity of something the primary Greek word rendered glory is *doxa* which really speaks to the perception of something as being good. The word is rendered glory

147 times also appearing as glorious, honor, praise and dignities. The closely related word *doxazo* really means to render glorious and is thus usually rendered glorified, glorify, or glorifying although it is rendered as glory on three occasions.

The word glory also appears in the rendering of *kenodoxos* although here the meaning is vain glory, or glorying when there is no reason to.

The Greek also has a family of words kauchaomai meaning 'boast' (verb), kauchē̄ma meaning that which causes boasting and kauchē̄sis the act of boasting. The former is rendered 'glory' one twenty occasions; the others upon three and one occasions respectively.

When not rendered as glory they are rendered as boasting or rejoicing.

A particularly vicious extension of this family is the word katakauchaomai which means to glory to the detriment of another; it appears once in James 3:14:

'But if ye have bitter envying and strife in your hearts, glory not, and lie not against the truth.'

It thus appears that these words fall between the Hebrew ha^lal which focuses rather more upon the positive nature of the subject and sha^bach which focuses somewhat more upon the mode of communication (speech).

We therefore see that in the New Testament the notion of Glory is much narrower and more focused than in the Old.

Further that focus is in the area that is the least prominent in the Hebrew. The Hebrew focuses upon volume and presence and only begins to move into the perception of something as glorious. In the New Testament the focus is upon the perception of something as having worth with an almost tangential and relatively minor move into the field of the proclamation of something as having worth whether or not it actually does."

Notice the last two paragraphs here as they relate to the usage of the word *glory* in the Old Testament and the New Testament. We must understand the importance of God's glory as it relates to His presence and is emphasized in the New Testament, but we must also understand the heaviness and power that God's glory brings when His presence is manifested. Knowing this should cause us to really want His glory to show up every time in our services.

"Worship is what we were created for. This is the final end of all existence—the worship of God. God created the universe so that it would display the worth of His glory. And He created us so that we would see this glory and reflect it by knowing and loving it—with all our heart and soul and mind and strength. The church needs to build a common vision of what worship is and what she is gathering to do on Sunday morning and scattering to do on Monday morning."

~ John Piper ~

True Worship Is an Experience Not an Event

"Worship is an it-is-well-with-my-soul experience."

~ Robert Webber ~

There has been too much personality and performance but not enough "presence" in the house of God. Ironically, in most of our churches today, we have more planned events and less of the authentic experiences and presence of God. When you come to the house of God, you should experience a tangible presence on a regular basis. I strongly believe that not only must there be strong teaching in the area of praise and worship but there also has to be an impartation of praise and worship.

For too long our churches have been social events; places we just hang out and where we meet people. Church is more than an event or something that we just do. Sadly, many only impose on the presence of God when we really need Him. We tend to praise Him when we feel like it, or when we think it's enough time spent in worship, we often stop prematurely!

To experience God is nothing like this world has to offer. The worship leader Matt Redman's song says it like this: "Better is one day in Your courts. Better is one day in Your house. Better is one day in your courts than a thousand elsewhere!"

A Life-Changing Experience

"And as he journeyed, he came near Damascus: and suddenly there shined round about him a light from heaven: And he fell to the earth, and heard a voice saying unto him, Saul, Saul, why persecutest thou me? And he said, Who art thou, Lord? And the Lord said, I am Jesus whom thou persecutest: it is hard for thee to kick against the pricks. And he trembling and astonished said, Lord, what will thou have me to do? And the Lord said unto him, Arise, and go into the city, and it shall be told thee what thou must do." Acts 9:3–6

Saul of Tarsus was known as one who always persecuted the church for the gospel's sake. However, one day he was on his way to persecute them and he had an encounter and conversation with the Lord. This is a tremendous example of an experience. It was more than an event. It was an experience that was the beginning of changing Saul's life forever. He eventually has an awakening in his spirit, a name change, and an appointment by God. He was transformed from Saul the Persecutor to the Apostle Paul.

This is what I call a life-changing experience. When you enter into the presence of a Holy God, who reveals all of His mercy and grace towards you, then and only then is there a heart change. An event will change your mind, but an experience will change your heart forever. So much happens when we really get to know Him. Destiny is discovered during these types of experiences.

I remember growing up in a religious setting, and there were always programs and special services, but what I didn't see was where God was on the program. It's amazing that in most denominations they have all kinds of events but still fail to acknowledge the Creator by allowing His authentic presence in. Coming up in the early years of my salvation, certain things were taboo in church. There was no real outpouring of the presence of God. People were leaving church the same way they came in.

There's something wrong with that! I believe that when we enter into the house of God, there should be signs and wonders. However, over the years I've discovered that some people really don't want the presence. They want the power, but they don't want the experience of a true encounter. They want the event and not the event planner.

It's almost like the bigger some of our churches become, the smaller God becomes. You must understand that numbers have never moved God. It is the quality of the heart that He pays attention to.

I have been in so many different church settings, and it never ceases to amaze me how we can become a regimented, systematic, closed-minded group of individuals who just want a part of God when it's convenient.

Let's take, for example, Romans chapter 10, when Paul talks about the prayer of salvation. For some, that's only an event; for others, it's just the beginning of experiencing God every day in their lives. God never intended for us to stop at the prayer of salvation. He purposed for us to have the Holy Spirit, who would lead us into deeper dimensions so that we could experience the God kind of life!

~ 51 ~

Most of our churches today are full of people that have an event with God instead of an experience. This is why we have more people running away from God instead of running to God. An intimate experience with God will give you the depth to endure trials and tribulations.

The Latin meaning of the word *endure* is "harden like steel."

Your worship experience can give you the strength to survive any hardship that you might have to endure.

When you really have an encounter with God, you will know for certain how real He is and how much He loves you. I have been in services time and time again where I have seen people having a worship experience for real. They were lying out prostrate before the Lord; weeping and crying, hands raised; they were focused on the presence of God. The spirit of God was hovering over that place like a blanket, and the people were basking in the experience.

"Deep calleth unto deep at the noise of thy waterspouts: all thy waves and thy billows are gone over me." Psalm 42:7

We need more of an experience in worship in our services. People's lives and destinies are weighing in the balance. Sadly, we have missed it here in the body of Christ for decades. I just declare that God is raising up a nation of people who want more of God; more than the Sunday event or the weekday event. These are people that want more of Him all the time!

I declare that there will be an emergence of the Davids and people that will long for the raw presence of God—the restructuring and rebuilding of the tabernacles of David; a release of the Key of David in the Earth that will turn and shift this generation to the heart of the father. I declare a new breed, a kingdom-minded culture that will shock the foundations of the spirit of religion. The presence of God will move in such a way that many would come to know Him who knew not religion. For many have known me through religion says the Lord, but the generation of now will know me by relationship. For they have not been tainted by doctrines and sayings of men. For where I shift, they will shift. What I release, they will release in the earth with a passion for me says the Lord.

I see the young lions are stirring in the spirit. For the time of the great awakening is upon us. The lions are coming to the church says the Lord. The lions are coming! This sound will be heard near and far. For others will hear a distinct sound and come out of hiding. For many have been waiting for the roar of thunder, the sound of worship to shake the heavens and release sons and daughters in the earth. So get ready says the Lord. The great awakening is upon us… This generation will reveal My glory in such a way says the Lord. I sense a momentum shift!

Try God

It's often been stated that experience is the best teacher. In this case, I believe it. When you try Him for yourself, you'll never want to go back. He's more than just goose bumps and your hair standing up on your back. He's Yahweh, the Creator, your King of kings and Lord of lords.

"Jesus said, 'Everyone who drinks this water will get thirsty again and again. Anyone who drinks the water I give will never thirst—not ever. The water I give will be an artesian spring within, gushing fountains of endless life.'" John 4:13–14 (The Message)

"You must understand that songs that change lives are songs that are birthed with a burden."

~ Tom Bynum ~

Chamber Two

True Worship Requires Humility & Submission

"The recipe for worship is humility, obedience, and sensitivity." ~ Unknown ~

Humility and total submission have to be instilled and in place as a foundation for every church organization or ministry. A church worship ministry full of Indian chiefs becomes a big issue. There should be only one chief per tribe.

Those that lead worship must demonstrate humility in their service to the worship ministry as well as towards God.

"The fear of the LORD is the instruction of wisdom; and before honour is humility." Proverbs 15:33

"Which things have indeed a shew of wisdom in will worship, and humility, and neglecting of the body: not in any honour to the satisfying of the flesh." Colossians 2:23

Humility in its simplest form is denying self in order to obey God and work as a team member. In a worship team setting, for example, even though it is made up of all Christians, there has to be an attitude of humility to work with all the different personalities.

Our goal and objective should always be to lead God's people to His presence. There should not be a competitive spirit but a spirit of unity. It's a pleasant thing when we dwell in unity on one accord. Having a sense of congruency regarding cohesiveness allows the Spirit of the Lord to move more effectively.

"Behold, how good and how pleasant it is for brethren to dwell together in unity!" Psalm 133:1

"Endeavouring to keep the unity of the Spirit in the bond of peace." Ephesians 4:3

"Till we all come in the unity of the faith, and of the knowledge of the Son of God, unto a perfect man, unto the measure of the stature of the fullness of Christ: That we henceforth be no more children, tossed to and fro, and carried about with every wind of doctrine, by the sleight of men, and cunning craftiness, whereby they lie in wait to deceive; But speaking the truth in love, may grow up into him in all things, which is the head, even Christ: From whom the whole body fitly joined together and compacted by that which every joint supplieth, according to the effectual working in the measure of every part, maketh increase of the body unto the edifying of itself in love." Ephesians 4:13–16

Paul makes a very valid statement by pointing out how important it is to walk together in love because we all have a part to play in advancing the Kingdom. We must walk in peace and not be distracted by petty, mediocre things that pull the attention away from God and put it on us.

Humility Brings Unity

We can and will see more increase of His presence and favor in our worship services than we've ever encountered before as we remember there is an order to praise and worship.

The fact is that God is the head and we are just an extension of Him playing our part in the earth realm to fulfill His divine will and purpose.

We can also learn from the principle and power of one accord that was demonstrated in the book of Acts on the day of Pentecost. There was a release of the presence and power of God. Explosive and dynamite power! (Acts 2)

We can conquer so much more when we flow in congruence with one another. It becomes more difficult when pride comes into play and we want to steal the show.

"Pride goeth before destruction, and an haughty spirit before a fall." Proverbs 16:18

"A man's pride shall bring him low: but honour shall uphold the humble in spirit." Proverbs 29:23

We all should remember the story of the worship leader in heaven, Lucifer, whose name also meant Morning Star and Shining One. The name Lucifer is translated here from the Hebrew word *helel,* which means "brightness." He had it all—the talent, position, and respect—but he lost it all because of one reason: pride!

This has become the outcome of many worship leaders, pastors, and musicians. Be careful because God will remove you and appoint and raise up someone else!

Here are seven enemies to humility that you must guard against:

1. Ambition – a desire to have worth

2. Selfishness – one's own interests

3. Deception – persuasion based on false information

4. Pride – subscribing to your own program

5. Rebellion – a disregard for authority

6. Stubbornness – a disregard for correction

7. Reprobate Thinking – cannot make godly choices

(*Wisdom Insights* by Bishop I. V. Hilliard)

What's Your Heart's Attitude?

"Let us come before His presence with thanksgiving, and make a joyful noise unto him with psalms." Psalm 95:2

When it comes to leading praise and worship, it must be a part of you. You must put God first above all else. Revealing Jesus to the world is what it's all about. We can reveal God as we authentically express a heart of humble worship to Him.

If you are trying to lead for all of the wrong reasons, you will be found out by man and exposed by God. The order starts when your desire is to have godly intentions.

Why do you want to be a part of the worship ministry? Is it really for you?

You can find the answers to these questions by asking yourself another, even more vital question:

Can you still maintain your passion if you have to worship alone in your private time without ever having an opportunity to stand before people?

If you can do it at home in private, certainly you can do it in public. It doesn't work the other way around; public first, then private.

I can remember years ago at the church I was saved at, how I was called upon as a teenager to lead what used to be called testimony service. This was a time when we would sing spontaneous praises to God with brief moments of impromptu testimonies from the congregation. I was young in the Lord and just glad to be saved. I was totally okay with worshipping God behind the scenes and hiding in the crowd.

Then one day one of my spiritual mothers at that time, Juanita Cotton, beckoned me to come forth and take the lead. I was hesitant and uncertain, but after that day, I realized that there was such an honor and blessing to be used by God to lead His people in worship like that. Since that day until now, I have not stopped in my public or private worship.

When it comes to being a real worshipper, you must remember that you don't choose your gifting and calling; you discover it.

God chooses it! If you are a worship leader, the reality is you can probably find many other better, more talented and experienced worship leaders than yourself. But that is not what God is looking for. Just like David was called upon to be king over his brothers, God will call those who He desires to lead worship because He's looking at the attitude of the heart. Everyone, including David's own father, overlooked him. But when favor is on you, it's on you! I make this statement quite often, and it's very true:

> "You have been chosen to be overlooked but noticed to be next."

There is a season of insignificance that you must go through in order to be proven. But you better believe when you stand the test of time, you will be ripe for the harvest of opportunities that will be before you.

You Can't Appoint Yourself

"And these are they whom David set over the service of song in the house of the LORD, after that the ark had rest. And they ministered before the dwelling place of the tabernacle of the congregation with singing, until Solomon had built the house of the LORD in Jerusalem: and then they waited on their office according to their order." 1 Chronicles 6:31–32

"And he appointed, according to the order of David his father, the courses of the priests to their service, and the Levites to their charges, to praise and minister before the priests, as the duty of every day required: the porters also by their courses at every gate: for so had David the man of God commanded." 2 Chronicles 8:14

Notice here that the leaders did not set their own position or appoint themselves. They were under an established order that they followed.

Submission Brings Order

For the most part in our local church worship services where I pastor and am the head worship leader, we have a lot of diversity in the way we function and flow. In most of our worship services, it is standard that we sing a couple of fast praise songs first and then eventually get to the slow worship songs.

There is nothing in stone to say this "has" to be the order though. The order of the kingdom is to be ready, willing, and able to sing slow if God says sing slow and sing fast if He says go fast. If He says, "Praise me for the entire service," then that's what we do.

The first true step to any worship team or worship ministry flowing together is to SUBMIT to the Holy Spirit's leading. You will encounter such a greater glory. I'm talking about like when Moses came down from Mt. Sinai. The glory was evident! The order is not to shut the worship service down when it "seems" to be getting out of control. Sometimes God is really moving on and through His people. Emotional healing, deliverance, and breakthroughs can start manifesting. The spirit of the breaker can come in the house!

"The breaker is come up before them: they have broken up, and have passed through the gate, and are gone out by it: and their king shall pass before them, and the LORD on the head of them." Micah 2:13

Avoiding the Spooky!

Now understand me; I know there will be times when you'll have spooky stuff, crazy stuff, and some of what you can't explain happening with people at times. Every church has that weird crowd. That's okay because things get kind of messy when breakthrough is happening. Just make sure you have systems in place to monitor the service without quenching the Spirit. Remember, you can't just let folks rule your house and act crazy with an attention-getting spirit.

Also, I'm not saying release your house to worship and stay in service all night. It won't take God that long to do what He needs to do. If it takes longer, it's because of us!

What I am saying is that there is a submission that we must operate under based on timing in our services. You have to know when it's the right time to shift to another pace of songs or even if you're to stay where you are. The order of every worship team and ministry should be to have their ear connected to the voice of God and their heart connected to heaven. This prevents the spirit of error from intruding an imposing on the service.

"And when he putteth forth his own sheep, he goeth before them, and the sheep follow him: for they know his voice. And a stranger will they not follow, but will flee from him: for they know not the voice of strangers." John 10:4-5

In our services today, we have people that follow everything and anything except the spirit of God. There is always an order, and it's discovered through humility and submission!

Connect with the Song

Don't sing songs your heart can't connect with; songs that are beyond your depth of spirituality. Just because you heard someone else sing a song and saw the results they got does not mean you can tap into that same realm. You may think, "Man I need to learn that song." Wrong! Every song may not be for you or your church.

For some this may be the case, but not all. It is important as a worship team and leader that you first connect with the song. Don't wait until it's time to lead to try and "be deep." People will know you don't really know what you're singing about.

Take the Limits Off

Let's not limit ourselves to a 10-minute encounter with God. Every now and then you may need to give Him 30 minutes, an hour, or as long as it takes. Praise and worship fits you well. It's just your size.

I promise when you get in a certain place in life, where it's rough, the order for your day will become praise with a side order of worship!

"And they came to the place which God had told him of; and Abraham built an altar there, and laid the wood in order, and bound Isaac his son, and laid him on the altar upon the wood." Genesis 22:9

God gave Abraham specific instructions in this passage of Scripture. Sometimes his instructions won't make sense; but they do make faith! We never know how the spirit of God

~ 65 ~

will move. But we must adapt and adjust so we can be in His will.

I can only imagine how hard the decision was that Abraham had to make as he was instructed to go up to the mountain and worship God by sacrificing his only son.

Sometimes God will test your worship to see if it's for real. Just like Abraham, God will provide you a ram in the bush when you give Him the sacrifice of praise and your heart is to worship Him.

"And they shall come from the cities of Judah, and from the places about Jerusalem, and from the land of Benjamin, and from the plain, and from the mountains, and from the south, bringing burnt offerings, and sacrifices, and meat offerings, and incense, and **bringing sacrifices of praise**, unto the house of the LORD." Jeremiah 17:26

God will do something big as you follow his order of worship. He will provide you a ram in the bush. You must continue to present your life, your body, and your heart to God and see if He won't bless you indeed just like His servant Abraham. You must remember that God is not a respecter of a person, but He does respect principles.

"The devil sees nothing more abominable than a truly humble Christian, for [that Christian] is just the opposite of [the devil's] own image."

~ Hans Nielsen Hauge ~

TRUTH #6

Praise Is a Weapon

"Praising God will seriously damage your problems."

~Unknown ~

"I will bless the LORD at all times: his praise shall continually be in my mouth." Psalm 34:1

As a believer, I challenge you to make this confession:

"I will not have God have to come looking for my praise, but I will bring my praise to Him every chance I get!"

The word *praise* in the Greek is *aineo,* which denotes simply "to praise."

"So he, leaping up, stood and walked and entered the temple with them—walking, leaping, and praising God." Acts 3:8 (NKJV)

Often praise and worship are believed to be the same, but they are not. *Praise* involves thanking God for all the things He's done and going to do for you. *Worship,* however, involves thanking God for who He is!

If He never does another thing for you— pays another bill for you, heals your body, and so forth—He's still Jehovah; He's still Yaweh; He's still Adonai; and He's still your God.

Praise, according to Webster's dictionary, is: "words that express approval or admiration for someone's achievements or someone's good qualities. It also means to applaud or to magnify, the word magnify in the Greek is *megaluno*, "to make or declare great, increase or extol, enlarge, magnify, show great." In other words:

To praise God is to make Him bigger than anything else in your life!

"Praise ye the LORD; for it is good to sing praises unto our God; for it is pleasant; and praise is comely." Psalm 147:1

The Midnight Praise

Praise is an expression of faith and a declaration of victory.

"And at midnight Paul and Silas prayed, and sang praises unto God: and the prisoners heard them. And suddenly there was a great earthquake, so that the foundations of the prison were shaken: and immediately all the doors were opened, and everyone's bands were loosed." Acts 16:25–26

Now, I had to use this story of Paul and Silas to state a case here. Believe it or not, your praise has an effect on you and your situation. Paul and Silas could have said, "That's it. We are about to die; our life is over." Suffice to say they did the opposite even though they were in jail and it was midnight. Midnight implies a hopeless situation, yet they began to praise God.

There had to be a shift in the mind first before the shift could occur in the natural. Something happened in that jail cell; not only were Paul and Silas affected but all the other prisoners as well. They found out that their doors were now opened and that they were free. True praise from deep down, or should I say as worship leader Eddie James calls it a "Nazarite cry," will spread like wildfire, and others around you will be affected.

Now understand here: The devil would always love for us to stay focused on our problems, become complacent, or even just lie down and accept fate. But I declare unto you the devil is a liar, and you must ensure that he stays that way.

Don't let trials and tribulations affect your praise!

Your praise is potential dynamite ready to explode in the face of the devil. All it takes is just one match to start a fire. Your praise and worship to God can be the match that sets your entire church on fire!

In his blog post, "O to Be a Prophet," on Identity Network's website, Kim Clement says this:

> "Praise to God is the most unselfish act that a human being can perform, especially when they are experiencing various kinds of pain and upset. There is a sentence used in the Bible that describes the highest form of praise to God. It is an honor that was granted to the Levites and the Sons of Zadok (who were priests), and that honor was to 'minister to the Lord.' To minister to the Lord means 'to bless God, to congratulate Him, to honor Him for who He is, His eternal covenant and to bring gifts to Him.'
>
> It's all about giving to God, not receiving, and once this takes place, God always responds with blessings upon His people."

Your Praise is Intercessory Prayer

"Even them will I bring to my holy mountain, and make them joyful in my house of prayer: their burnt offerings and their sacrifices shall be accepted upon mine altar; for mine house shall be called an house of prayer for all people." Isaiah 56:7

In the New Testament, Jesus quotes in Matthew, Mark and Luke that His "house shall be called a house of prayer" (Matthew 21:13, Mark 11:17, Luke 19:46). According to Strong's Exhaustive Concordance the Hebrew word for prayer here in this scripture is *tĕphillah* and it is used seventy-seven times in the King James Version of the bible. Its biblical usage and meaning includes that of a poetic or liturgical prayer. The Gesenius' Hebrew-Chaldee Lexicon indicates one of the manners it is translated particularly signifies a hymn or a sacred song. Your praise is a form of prayer!

"Praise ye the LORD. Sing unto the LORD a new song, and his praise in the congregation of saints. Let Israel rejoice in him that made him: let the children of Zion be joyful in their King. Let them praise his name in the dance: let them sing praises unto him with the timbrel and harp. For the LORD taketh pleasure in his people: he will beautify the meek with salvation. Let the saints be joyful in glory: let them sing aloud upon their beds. Let the high praises of God be in their mouth, and a two-edged sword in their hand; To execute vengeance upon the heathen, and punishments upon the people; To bind their kings with chains, and their nobles with fetters of iron; To execute upon them the judgment written:

this honour have all his saints. Praise ye the LORD." Psalm 149

Your praise has the ability to execute vengeance upon the enemy; to punish him; to bind him; and to judge him!

Sow Your Praise for Breakthrough

"Give, and it shall be given unto you; good measure, pressed down, and shaken together, and running over, shall men give into your bosom. For with the same measure that ye mete withal it shall be measured to you again." Luke 6:38

When you hear Luke 6:38, what's the first thing that you think? Well, for most of us, it would be relative to finances. But let's look at this text from a broader viewpoint.

Giving, in Luke 6:38, could imply more than in the area of your finances. You can't out give God on anything! And when you praise Him, things are loosed for you.

"Out of the mouth of babes and sucklings hast thou ordained strength because of thine enemies, that thou mightest still the enemy and the avenger." Psalm 8:2

Giving praise to God confuses the enemy. It's literally as though now the devil is running in a circle because he doesn't know what to do.

Benefits of Praise

It is very important that we establish a life of praise. There are three benefits of praise for the believer:

1. Praise builds your faith. Our lifestyle of praise and thanksgiving increases our faith. Colossians 2:6–7:

   "As ye have therefore received Christ Jesus the Lord, so walk ye in him: Rooted and built up in him, and stablished in the faith, as ye have been taught, abounding therein with thanksgiving."

2. Praise defeats the devil.

3. Praise ministers to God.

When we praise and worship God, we shift our mind towards His promises and away from our problems.

Have you ever really praised God before and afterwards you felt so much better? You felt renewed and refreshed and even lighter. It's because your praise is a weapon, and the devil knows this. You need to get it together and just give God the praise.

I've heard it stated time and time again that praise will make room for more. Do you need more?

The amount of time we spend praising God demonstrates where we are in our relationship with Him.

Psalm 30:1–6: "I will extol thee, O LORD; for thou hast lifted me up, and hast not made my foes to rejoice over me. O LORD my God, I cried unto thee, and thou hast healed me. O LORD, thou hast brought up my soul from the grave: thou hast kept me alive, that I should not go down to the pit.

Sing unto the LORD, O ye saints of his, and give thanks at the remembrance of his holiness. For his anger endureth but a moment; in his favour is life: weeping may endure for a night, but joy cometh in the morning. And in my prosperity I said, I shall never be moved."

<u>Praise Gives God the Credit</u>

I love what David says here. He uses the word "extol." This is a word that is not used as often as it should be in our praise and worship services. It literally means to "give credit to." In this passage, David starts out giving God the credit. While he's praising God, he is consumed with the revelation that if it had not been for the Lord, he would still be down and out. When you are entering into praise to God, are you thinking thoughts like, "I wouldn't be here; I wouldn't be alive. I would've lost my mind. I would be in my grave today if it had not been for the Lord!"? Today I now know what the old mothers and fathers of the church meant when they made those types of statements.

Sow your praise and reap a harvest of breakthrough.

Edwin Hawkins penned a song years ago called "Thank You Lord":

"Tragedies are common place. All kinds of diseases; people are slipping away. Economics down, people can't get enough pay. But as for me all I can say is, Thank you Lord for all you've done for me."

That's it! A secret to turning around your situation is opening up your mouth and giving the credit to the Lord for your blessings! I believe we make the devil so mad when in spite of all we are going through or have been through we keep on praising God. I call that an "in spite of praise"! Even right now, if you would take a moment to reflect on the mercy, grace, and goodness of God, you would praise Him as well. It's time to start giving credit where credit is due.

You know there wasn't anyone that could've gotten you out of that tight spot in your life but Him. Glory to God! I dare you right now to just take a break and give God an "anyhow and in spite of praise"! Go ahead confuse the devil. Make him regret he ever messed with your marriage, ministry, calling, finances, worship and praise services, or life. Extol and exalt the Lord! I dare you!

Praise Brings the Double

Just like Job, you are going to get double for all the trouble you had to endure. Remember, Job lost it all, but God restored back to him double because he maintained his attitude of devotion to the Lord!

I prophesy to you right now that as you lift up your hands and praise God, double is on its way: double grace, double favor, double increase, double land and real estate—double! Glory to God! Your turn around is here!

"For your shame ye shall have double; and for confusion they shall rejoice in their portion: therefore in their land they shall possess the double: everlasting joy shall be unto them." Isaiah 61:7

In your singing or shouting a song of praise, God will take it and birth uncommon events in your life.

<u>Praise Defeats Your Enemy</u>

Another great biblical example is that of Jehoshaphat. They had come out with unbelievable spoils. It is impossible to give God true praise and He not move on your behalf.

2 Chronicles 20:15–19, 22–23, 25:

"And he said, Hearken ye, all Judah, and ye inhabitants of Jerusalem, and thou king Jehoshaphat, Thus saith the LORD unto you, Be not afraid nor dismayed by reason of this great multitude; for the battle is not yours, but God's. To morrow go ye down against them: behold, they come up by the cliff of Ziz; and ye shall find them at the end of the brook, before the wilderness of Jeruel. Ye shall not need to fight in this battle: set yourselves, stand ye still, and see the salvation of the LORD with you, O Judah and Jerusalem: fear not, nor be dismayed; tomorrow go out against them: for the LORD will be with you. And Jehoshaphat bowed his head with his face to the ground: and all Judah and the inhabitants of Jerusalem fell before the LORD, worshipping the LORD. And the Levites, of the children of the Kohathites, and of the children of the Korhites, stood up to praise the LORD God of Israel with a loud voice on high. And when they began to sing and to praise, the LORD set ambushments against the children of Ammon, Moab, and mount Seir, which were come against Judah; and they were smitten. For the children of Ammon and Moab stood up against the inhabitants of mount Seir, utterly to slay and destroy them: and when they had made an end of the inhabitants of Seir, every one helped to destroy another. And when Jehoshaphat and his people came to take away the spoil of them, they found among them in abundance both riches with the dead bodies, and precious jewels, which they stripped off for themselves, more than they could carry away: and they were three days in gathering of the spoil, it was so much."

I love what one of my spiritual fathers, Bishop I. V. Hilliard, says on the subject of the Benefits of Praise:

1. It stifles the enemy.
2. It brings a sense of God's presence on the scene.
3. It releases you from emotional bondage.
4. It brings deliverance.
5. It causes God to defend my rights.
6. It triggers the supernatural.
7. It places you in God's protective custody program.

Praise Is a Commandment

"Let us hear the conclusion of the whole matter; Fear God, and keep His commandments; for this is the whole duty of man. For God shall bring every work into judgment, with every secret thing, whether it be good, or whether it be evil." Ecclesiastes 12:13–14

"Let everything that hath breath praise the LORD. Praise ye the LORD." Psalm 150:6

"I think we delight to praise what we enjoy because the praise not merely expresses but completes the enjoyment; it is its appointed consummation." ~ C.S. Lewis ~

Praise & Worship Has a Tribe

"We are the gateway to heaven on earth! God uses humanity to speak the things that He's gonna do on the earth."

~ Trent Cory ~

"And she conceived again, and bare a son: and she said, Now will I praise the LORD: therefore she called his name Judah; and left bearing." Genesis 29:35

"And the children of Israel arose, and went up to the house of God, and asked counsel of God, and said, Which of us shall go up first to the battle against the children of Benjamin? And the LORD said, Judah shall go up first." Judges 20:18

The Bible speaks of 12 tribes of Israel, and out of the 12, the tribe of Judah stands out as being the one associated with the word praise. This tribe was known as the tribe that went up first in battle.

It should also be noted that the lion is the symbol of the tribe of Judah, and that is why it is often represented in Jewish art. Also, throughout the centuries, the church has associated the lion with Judah due to its distinct sound and a sense of authority.

As we study the tribe of Judah, we find that at its height, it was the leading tribe of the Kingdom of Judah, and it even occupied most of the territory of the kingdom. After the reign of Solomon, his son Rehoboam ruled in his place, and the Kingdom of Israel fell into great conflict and was divided in two; the northern kingdom more commonly known as Israel with the ten tribes of Rueben, Simeon, Dan, Naphtali, Gad, Asher, Issachar, Zebulun, Joseph (Ephraim and Manasseh), and Levi; and the Kingdom of Judah in the south made up of two tribes—Judah and Benjamin (1 Kings 11:29–39). Later, Levi left the northern kingdom and came to Judah as well (2 Chronicles 11:14).

The word Jew is a derivative of the word Judah, referring to a descendant of the Kingdom of Judah, though a Jew could also be a descendant of Benjamin or Levi.

Who's in the Tribe?

Now, just like there were 12 tribes of Israel that were distinctive, we all have distinctive gifts, and it is important to know which area God has gifted you in. You must KNOW and OPERATE in the area that God has gifted you in.

Although not everyone is assigned to lead worship, everyone has been assigned to participate in it.

Some of the distinctions within the tribe of Judah fall under the worship leaders. There is a difference between the psalmist (worship leader) and the minstrel (musician).

"And when Jesus came into the ruler's house, and saw the minstrels and the people making a noise..." Matthew 9:23

The "minstrels" here in Matthew 9:23 were the flute-players that were employed as professional mourners.

The Greek word for *minstrel* is *mousikos*—musical (as a noun), a minstrel, musician. The *minstrel* has the job of pulling the sound out of heaven that needs to be played upon the instrument. Minstrels must be skilled to flow under the unction of the Holy Spirit. The minstrel has to have the ability to assist the psalmist in shifting the atmosphere.

The *psalmist* likewise has a very important job within the tribe. According to the dictionary, a psalmist is a composer of "sacred songs."

The psalmist has the ability to carry the song in a service and navigate it to its appropriate destination in the hearts of man and the throne room of God.

They have the responsibility of pulling words and even tunes out of the heavens just like the minstrel pulls the sounds and tunes out of the heavens. When the psalmist and the minstrel flow together with the words and sounds that are from the heavens, the glory of the Lord shows up!

"Also the Levites which were the singers, all of them of Asaph, of Heman, of Jeduthun, with their sons and their brethren, being arrayed in white linen, having cymbals and psalteries and harps, stood at the east end of the altar, and with them an hundred and twenty priests sounding with trumpets. It came even to pass, as the trumpeters and singers were as one, to make one sound to be heard in praising and thanking the LORD; and when they lifted up their voice with the trumpets and cymbals and instruments of musick, and praised the LORD, saying, For he is good; for his mercy endureth for ever: that then the house was filled with a cloud, even the house of the LORD; So that the priests could not stand to minister by reason of the cloud: for the glory of the LORD had filled the house of God." 2 Chronicles 5:12–14

Judah & the Culture

"Worship songs can't just be rooted in culture—they won't be deep enough. They have to be rooted in scripture."

~ Matt Redman ~

There is such a power and an influence that music has on us as a culture that it can drive men to love and it can drive them to hate and commit all kinds of atrocities. This is why it is important for the true psalmists and minstrels to come forth from the body of Christ.

In order for them to operate in authority, however, they will have to submit themselves under the authority of the Holy Spirit. It is my prayer that psalmists and minstrels would operate under the submission of the Holy Spirit and subject themselves under the set authority of their local house as well, just as those who were appointed by David in 1 Chronicles 25:1–3:

"Moreover David and the captains of the host separated to the service of the sons of Asaph, and of Heman, and of Jeduthun, who should prophesy with harps, with psalteries, and with cymbals: and the number of the workmen according to their service was: Of the sons of Asaph; Zaccur, and Joseph, and Nethaniah, and Asarelah, the sons of Asaph under the hands of Asaph, which prophesied according to the order of the king. Of Jeduthun: the sons of Jeduthun;

Gedaliah, and Zeri, and Jeshaiah, Hashabiah, and Mattithiah, six, under the hands of their father Jeduthun, who prophesied with a harp, to give thanks and to praise the LORD."

Notice here how King David appointed and delegated certain parts of the service. There were distinctive roles in which everyone had to play within the tribe.

The Mark of a Minstrel

The mark of a true minstrel includes the following:

- True minstrels understand the importance of being submitted to both spiritual and natural authority.
- True minstrels are punctual and prophetic in nature.
- True minstrels are not after money and material things.
- True minstrels are after the sound of heaven, the heart of worship, and the heart of God.
- True minstrels are more than skillful musicians; they are worshippers whose hearts, hands, and ears are in tune with heaven.

The best way I can sum this all up is that a Musician is for a Profit but the Minstrel is for the Prophet!

The Worship Leader

There are many worship leaders who are simply just that— worship leaders waiting to lead God's people. However, a worship leader must move from just being a worship leader to being a psalmist. They can only do this if they have a lifestyle of a worshipper. If they do not, it will eventually be realized by others.

Worship for a worship leader cannot just be on Sundays or maybe just one other day out of the week. It must be every day. It must be who you are. If a worship leader can't do it at home, then they have no business fronting before the people in the church.

When a worship leader gets to know God for themselves, the people will benefit from the overflow of their time spent with Him.

I have observed that some worship leaders don't have the passion to lead; some are just "fillers." They just like to sing. Others just like to be seen and are up in the front for attention.

True worship leaders are psalmists that are the best examples along with the other leaders in the church, including the pastor, as to what a worshipper should be and do.

The Mark of a Psalmist

The mark of a true psalmist can be seen by the following:

- They must have an ear to the throne room of God and can listen as He is releasing songs in the Earth.
- They must be in tune with the worship service EVEN WHEN THEY ARE NOT LEADING. (I have seen worship leaders as well as musicians folding their arms, looking around during worship; chewing gum;

having a conversation during worship; or even just simply looking not interested, as though they wish they were somewhere else! This is an absolute NO-NO!)

- They must have a strong awareness of who God is.
- They must have a strong sense of identity and know who they are in God.

As a psalmist or a minstrel, you don't have time for spinning your wheels and going through an identity crisis in life. This is the season of your life when you need to know where you belong and who you are.

You see, I found out something: We oftentimes set out to become one thing, but it's the plan of the Lord that will ultimately prosper. You must remember that your life is not determined by you but it's discovered by you. After a couple of seasons of going through, being down and sometimes out, you will begin to start discovering things about your life.

King David was a great example of both a psalmist and a minstrel who knew his identity. He knew who he was even when his dad Jesse didn't know who he was. The Bible even calls him a man after the heart of God.

When it comes to praise and worship, psalmists and minstrels must be SKILLED, SENSITIVE, and SELECTED.

Get the Tribe in Order

I made the statement once that when it comes down to the sound that is in a (church) house, it's often contingent upon the vessels that are willing to follow the sound and vision of that set house.

I firmly believe that in this season within praise and worship, we will see an unveiling and awakening of the sound of heaven. If you are truly a psalmist or a minstrel, one who is called to lead God's people in worship, then you are of the tribe of Judah!

True psalmists and minstrels will minister under authority and won't just do what they want to do. They won't try to hijack the service. They know how to take the people in with precision and anointing and position them in a place where their hearts are pliable and ready for the Word of God.

You must stay in your place and fine tune your gift. There are those that are gifted in so many other areas of ministry. It doesn't make anyone less significant. We all have a part to play, and we all need each other. Don't try and do it all and be it all. I know some people think they have it all. You don't!

I might get in trouble for this, but it must be said! We need to learn how to let our worship teams and leaders be proven before they are placed in position. Some churches make it too easy for people to assume leadership roles just because they heard a pretty voice sing. They can have a pretty voice, but they might be the devil in disguise because of the way they are living their lives.

Their lives can be totally out of order: They are not tithers or financial supporters of the ministry, or they might even be practicing sin—like being actively involved in fornication or the abuse of substances. Now, I know no one's perfect, but there should be godly criteria set in place that models its standards based on the Word of God. They should be accountable to God and submitted to the covering they are under.

Pastor and worship team leader, don't be deceived because you are desperate, but be determined to have discipline on your team.

Called to Lead Worship?

You want to know how you can know for sure that you've been called to lead worship? There will be an uncontrollable desire for the things of God that music alone can't take the place of.

You must have a desire or passion to see people experience God.

While you are sitting in services and the anointing is present, you hear melodies in your spirit. Then God might begin showing you glimpses of yourself standing before people singing as folks are being healed and delivered. Maybe God will start confirming His Word through other ministry gifts or prophets in the body of Christ.

You might go through a season where you are in worship service and something is revealed to you about how the worship can go deeper and be more intimate with God. Of course, this is not being judgmental by any means, but you just have a vision for more. You begin to see the potholes and roadblocks in the worship service and how they can be repaired with a yielded vessel leading the way.

In your spirit, things start connecting! You start becoming more intimate with God and spend more time with Him; the seed of worship is birthed in you out of the time you spend with Him. Music becomes who you are in the morning, afternoon, and evening. You wake up and the song of the Lord is in your mouth or on your heart.

Worship Tribes Throughout History

I have found out in music that there are so many variables to complete a distinct sound and that it is essential to stay connected to God in order to hear that sound.

There have been many different types of sounds throughout history that have released "moves of God" in the Earth realm. There also have been different types or movements of worship tribes throughout history. I really want you to see how music has changed according to the times and seasons. Every so often there's a thrust or shift in music that influences a generation. All throughout church history we can see this being documented and verified as the culture changes.

The following has been adapted from Wikipedia, the free Encyclopedia, "Contemporary Worship Music":

In the 1950s and '60s some Christians felt that the Church needed to break from its stereotype as being structured, formal, and dull to appeal to the younger generation. The Church abroad began to place particular emphasis on reaching the youth. In particularly, the Catholic Taizé Community in France started to attract young people from several religious denominations by using their worship hymns along with modern melodies.

Something I learned even in fishing is if you want to catch certain kinds of fish you must have a certain kind of bait. And as a side note, this is why we have all types of activities that transpire at our youth events in our local church; from the stepping, to the hip-hop music, and dancing for the Lord. I believe it is all relevant.

This openness of the Church to see its youth impacted was the beginning of a tremendous shift. This shift can even be traced back to the beginning of the charismatic movement of the 1960s. Contemporary worship came on the scene and became very popular because of its relevancy.

Contemporary worship, which is defined by songs that are frequently referred to as *praise songs* or *worship songs* and are typically led by a *worship band* or *praise team*, with either a guitarist or pianist leading, began to replace the traditional order of worship based around singing hymns out of worship books with extended periods of congregational singing.

As we look further back in history, it has been documented that a group by the name of *The Joystrings* was one of the first Christian pop groups to sing on television wearing Salvation Army uniforms and playing Christian beat music. During this time, the *Jesus People Movement* also came to the forefront.

Their hippie-style music was set to biblical lyrics and was often called *Jesus music*. This *Jesus music* eventually broke off to Christian rock, which was more commonly played for concerts, and praise music, which was primarily for communal worship.

As the worship music in the church continued to evolve during the late 1970s and early 1980s, the *Jesus People Movement* eventually began to phase out.

In came the '80s and '90s, where there was a transitioning from traditional to a more contemporary urban kind of music. The shift from gospel to more praise and worship began. Then in the late '90s, I remember there was a thrust in prophetic praise and worship, which many called the *Prophetic Worship Movement*.

As the culture of our music in the church continues to evolve, we are hearing a different style, a radical sound, and a cutting edge culture of people coming forth. Not only is the sound changing, but our methods of projecting this sound are also. We are freer to sing and express ourselves physically as many churches adapt modern technology into its worship. We are displaying our songs on screens with projectors; praise dancers minister in dance throughout the sanctuary; and Christian artists make creations as inspired by the worship taking place. We are finding a greater degree of unity and liberty made available for those that are involved in the worship service.

Important propagators of Contemporary Worship Music today include Hillsong, Israel Houghton, Mercy Me, Jeremy

Camp, David & Nicole Binion, Casting Crowns, Trent Cory, David Crowder Band, Eddie James, Newsboys, Chris Tomlin, William McDowell, Matt Maher, B. J. Putnam, Third Day, and so many others. I think you get the point now, right?

Contemporary Worship and the Charismatic Movement

The charismatic movement is widely known for its emphasis on the Holy Spirit and the need for a personal encounter and relationship with God. As I often say, "It's about relationship and not religion-ship." This influence that the movement has had on contemporary worship can be heard in the words to the songs and most of the music that is played. Songs that utilize intimate and informal words like "you" and "I" instead of "we" and "God" are a great example of this.

Contemporary worship is not only centered around having a personal relationship with God but also a freedom of expression. We can hear a range of expressions from personal and intimate in songs like: "Open the Eyes of My Heart" (Michael W. Smith), "I'm Coming Back to the Heart of Worship" (Matt Redman), "Lord I Give You My Heart" (Hillsong), and "I Give Myself Away" (William McDowell); to songs with slang in them: "We wanna see you high and lifted up!" in songs like "Angels Cry" (William Murphy); and friendly songs, such as "I Am a Friend of God" (Israel Houghton). Full body worship is even encouraged as songs like "Freedom" (Eddie James) encourages the clapping of hands, shouting to God, and jumping.

The Jesus Culture Tribe

I have mentioned just a few of the songs and worship leaders that are being used by God, but now let's look at one of the most widely known movements that is taking place. There have been many different movements that have come on the scene in the church regarding worship. Many have attempted but only a few have been successful in creating a lasting movement in the area of worship. One particular movement that has come to the forefront over the last decade is a movement called *Jesus Culture*.

According to Wikipedia, the free encyclopedia online:

> "*Jesus Culture* is an international Christian revivalist youth outreach ministry based at the Bethel Church of Redding, California. Jesus Culture Ministry hosts conferences and operates a record label, *Jesus Culture Music*, to share its message and spread worship. Jesus Culture began in the summer of 1999, when the youth group at Bethel Church in Redding, California, led by youth pastor Banning Liebscher, launched the first Jesus Culture conference. The ministry has been called 'one of the most significant Christian movements in post-war America.'
>
> Youth worship leaders Kim Walker-Smith, Melissa How and Chris Quilala, long active with the youth group at Bethel Church in Redding, became the core of the Jesus Culture band. Jesus Culture states the purpose of music in their movement is to "ignite revival in the nations of the earth...compel the Body of Christ to radically abandon itself to a lifestyle of worship...and...encounter His extravagant love and raw power."
>
> Since 2006, the band has released a number of albums on the Jesus Culture Music label. Their 2011 album, *Awakening (Live from Chicago)*, appeared at #133 on the Canadian music charts.

The album was reviewed by *Christianity Today*, who critiqued that "…amps of staggering sound leave little room for thoughtful reflection or deliberate contemplation…."

Obviously this person from *Christianity Today* who made this last statement doesn't have a balanced relationship and revelation on the subject matter. Understand this: *Jesus Culture* is more than just a band name—it's a movement! It's a group of young people who get together with a passion and desire for the things of God.

Remember that there will always be resistance to change. People's opinions and insecurities will surface about things that are changing or on the verge of change. As a part of the Tribe of Judah, it may require a shout of praise, a distinct sound, or a radical move that shifts the atmosphere. You must be willing to do something that may make you and others feel uncomfortable.

I can't begin to elaborate on so many others who have said that certain styles of worship did not belong in the church. Turn the music down! Get that guitar out of here! Don't replace that organ with a keyboard!

The world is full of people that are entitled to their opinion. However, as people of the Most High God, we have to shift as He says shift or get left behind. People may judge you, but they cannot deny the results! My Grandma Nanny used to say, "The proof is in the pudding."

I have personally followed *Jesus Culture* for years now. They have proven time and time again a heart for God and His presence. There have been countless times where people have experienced a visitation and intimate moments as they began to worship. My life personally has been impacted by their sound and its presence.

Praise God for *Jesus Culture*! In this same flow, many others have really begun to surface more and more; such as Eddie James, Misty Edwards, Sean Feucht, Jason Upton, Heather Clark, the IHOP Movement in Kansas City, MO, with their around the clock worship sessions, Lydia Stanley, Roy Fields, and Kim Clement. All of these possess a sound for a generation now! One of my desires in this season of my life is to inspire a generation to worship and praise.

<u>We Must Change</u>

The church must understand that as the culture changes it must as well. Although we preach the same message of a risen Christ who has provided redemption for us all, we must utilize different methods in getting that message across. With every new generation, there's a sound change. Every generation that comes on the scene must ascertain the relevant aspects of God for their generation.

We must not try and put God in a box. He is multi-dimensional, and there is no one side to Him. God is always revealing another side of Himself as the generations evolve.

He has to do it this way because we could not take too much of Him all at once. It would be overwhelmingly impossible because He is so awesome!

Therefore, we must not seek to just challenge this generation to worship, but we must inspire them to worship on their level.

They must tap into worship on their own level. It may not be in the way you have been accustomed to. We must constantly remind ourselves of how the world around us is changing. Technology is changing every three to six months on average. That's how fast things are moving. Just like you don't want to be left behind when it comes to technology, you should not want to be left behind when it comes to worship.

There are people that will go out and buy the latest gadget in order to stay up to date with technology, but they are content with singing the same old worship hymns. Religion will cause you to keep doing the same thing even if it is not relevant or productive. It's because familiarity and comfort zones are breeding grounds for barrenness.

If you are in a church and there are a lot of youth, you must remember that they are into the "new sound." So you are going to have to make sure that you are tapping into this sound. There's no way around it. If you want to lose your youth, just stay in the past! We need the praise dancers, the steppers, the spoken word poet, and the young psalmists and prophets to be uninhibited spiritually!

Relevant Worship

If the likes of MTV and BET can capture the heart and attention of this generation, then the church has got to take it up a notch. After all, music originally emanated from heaven. It always belonged to God first.

It is up to the worship leaders and pastors to stay current with the new sound. I strongly believe that worship leaders should be responsible for knowing what's hot and what's not. What's current in the area of praise and worship? As a true worship leader, it should be natural for them to know the popular songs and music to contemporary praise and worship.

Now understand; I have nothing against the old hymns. I believe that there are times and seasons for Word-based and Spirit-led hymns as well as spiritual songs. But I have enough sense to know that in order to reach this generation and keep their attention, I must be flexible and open.

I understand that I can't lead a church that has an eight track player mentality in an iPod generation. Having a "Walkman" and "cassette" church ministry are not relevant either. It's important that when it comes to the sounds of heaven, your worship ministry must keep up with them and stay relevant! As a worship leader, staying on top of the top 10 worship songs is a great way to do this.

It's also important to note here that in your relevance, you don't remove the foundation. The basis for everything we do in the church is still always based on the Word of God. Music alone can't stand no matter how good it sounds or how relevant the words are to the culture.

The message of the Kingdom has not changed and will not change; however, it's the methods by which we reach this current generation that must be modified.

"Remove not the ancient landmark, which thy fathers have set." Proverbs 22:28

<u>Uniting for Change</u>

We don't want to be like the 12 tribes of Israel that split up; as a result of this disunity, they were open prey for the enemy to come in and devour them. So much power is made available when the body is unified in worship and praise. We need the corporate anointing in our services.

We must engage as the Tribe of Judah together as one voice with one sound. If you want to know more about someone or something, you must research its origin. In other words, you say you are a worship leader, minister, or leader in the church, etc., but, "Who did you come from? Who are you really connected to? Who are you really serving?"

There's always a lesson to learn in everything you go through. I am sure you have learned that when opinions, pride, and egos get in the way of things because of division, nations and people can be literally destroyed. Remember we are stronger together as believers than when we are apart.

The Tribe of Judah has the ability to confuse the enemy every time with praise. Judah has the responsibility of creating the atmosphere. There is no time for negativity! Our God is awesome, and we must proclaim this to the world through our worship!

Your praise can change your perspective, your outlook, and your take on life! It's time to be like the Lion of the Tribe of Judah! Let the song of the Lord come forth with a roar!

"Up with God! Down with his enemies! Adversaries, run for the hills! Gone like a puff of smoke, like a blob of wax in the fire—one look at God and the wicked vanish. When the righteous see God in action they'll laugh, they'll sing, they'll laugh and sing for joy. Sing hymns to God; all heaven, sing out; clear the way for the coming of Cloud-Rider. Enjoy GOD, cheer when you see him!" Psalms 68:1–1, The Message

"If we as worship leaders can get God's people into His presence, God will do the rest. The more we are exposed to His presence, the more we act like and reflect Him."

~ B.J. Putnam ~

Chamber Three

There Must Be a Distinctive Sound Released

"Everything in life follows the sound that it makes. You don't like the direction your life is heading?
Change the sound."
~ Apostle Ron Carpenter ~

The word *sound* denotes an announcement, a proclamation, or a noise; the sensation produced by stimulation of the organs of hearing by vibrations transmitted through the air or other medium.

"The speed of sound is the distance travelled during a unit of time by a sound wave propagating through an elastic medium. In dry air at 20 °C (68 °F), the speed of sound is 343.2 meters per second (1,126 ft/s). This is 1,236 kilometers per hour (768 mph), or about one kilometer in three seconds or approximately one mile in five seconds." (Wikipedia the Free Encyclopedia)

The amazing thing about a sound is that it has the ability to travel at light speed. Sound can even travel through barriers. Think about the many times when you are inside with all of the doors and windows closed yet you can hear what's going on outside.

The dynamics involving sound are simply incredible. It has the ability to get to a place faster than we can. For example, you can yell for help and that sound can arrive in another room (location) before you physically get there.

Another powerful thing about sound is that you don't have to see it to hear it and know that it is there! This is what demonstrates your faith. You don't have to see the house of your dreams with your natural eyes. You don't have to see the car in the physical. You don't have to see that you are debt free in the physical. But you can begin to see the breakthrough in your mind and speak the breakthrough with your mouth—make the sound.

Create the Sound

As you create the sound from your mouth and stop speaking negatively, you will have whatsoever you say! (Mark 11:23) If God can speak it and it comes to pass, so can you. Let's look at Genesis 1, where God spoke and what He spoke came into existence every single time.

Genesis 1:3 – "And God said, Let there be light: and there was light."

Genesis 1:6 – "And God said, Let there be a firmament in the midst of the waters, and let it divide the waters from the waters."

Genesis 1:9 – "And God said, Let the waters under the heaven be gathered together unto one place, and let the dry land appear: and it was so."

Genesis 1:11 – "And God said, Let the earth bring forth grass, the herb yielding seed, and the fruit tree yielding fruit after his kind, whose seed is in itself, upon the earth: and it was so."

Genesis 1:14 – "And God said, Let there be lights in the firmament of the heaven to divide the day from the night; and let them be for signs, and for seasons, and for days, and years:"

Genesis 1:20 – "And God said, Let the waters bring forth abundantly the moving creature that hath life, and fowl that may fly above the earth in the open firmament of heaven."

Genesis 1:24 – "And God said, Let the earth bring forth the living creature after his kind, cattle, and creeping thing, and beast of the earth after his kind: and it was so."

Genesis 1:26 – "And God said, Let us make man in our image, after our likeness: and let them have dominion over the fish of the sea, and over the fowl of the air, and over the cattle, and over all the earth, and over every creeping thing that creepeth upon the earth."

Genesis 1:28–29 – "And God blessed them, and God said unto them, Be fruitful, and multiply, and replenish the earth, and subdue it: and have dominion over the fish of the sea, and over the fowl of the air, and over every living thing that moveth upon the earth. And God said, Behold, I have given you every herb bearing seed, which is upon the face of all the earth, and every tree, in the which is the fruit of a tree yielding seed; to you it shall be for meat."

You must understand that there is authority released in your sound. You can literally call something out of a nothing situation. Now, think of this in the worship setting and how you have the ability with the sound you create to bring miracles into the atmosphere!

Let's look at the story of Abraham and Sarah. Sarah, medically speaking, was far beyond child-bearing years, but God wanted to work a miracle!

I love the fact that Abraham could've said, "You know what, Sarah, this ain't gonna happen girl! It's a hopeless situation. Girl, we ain't young like we used to be." But Abraham did the opposite.

He allowed a sound of praise to be released from his mouth because he stood in faith! Romans chapter 4 tells us that he was strong in faith and gave glory to God. Because if God said he was gonna do it, then it's gonna be! It's not up to me to try and figure it out! The old mothers in the church would say, "God's already worked it out!"

Romans 4:17–20:

"(As it is written, I have made thee a father of many nations,) before him whom he believed, even God, who quickeneth the dead, and calleth those things which be not as though they were. Who against hope believed in hope, that he might become the father of many nations, according to that which was spoken, So shall thy seed be. And being not weak in faith, he considered not his own body now dead, when he was about an hundred years old, neither yet the deadness of Sarah's womb: He staggered not at the promise of God through unbelief; but was strong in faith, giving glory to God;"

As a believer, you frame your own world; no one else can do that except you. As a worshipper, you have the ability to release a powerful sound that will change your atmosphere.

"Death and life are in the power of the tongue: and they that love it shall eat the fruit thereof." Proverbs 18:21

Remember, just like you can hear a train coming before you see it on the track and you can hear a plane coming before you see it in the sky, you must release a sound that can be heard before you see your miracle manifest. Before your release comes; before your increase comes; before your healing comes; you must change the atmosphere with your sound! The sound being released on your part validates the fact that you play a part in the process of your miracle coming to pass. I love what Bishop I. V. Hilliard says:

"God will not do anything in your life without first your participation."

<u>The Right Sound</u>

There are so many forms or ways to express our praise and worship to God. There is a vocal sound you make by your voice. There's a sound you make on an instrument, be it percussion or strings or horns.

When we have the right sound coming from our worship services, our prayers that have been on hold will be released! When the right sound is released in the worship service, the things that the people have been standing in faith for will begin to manifest.

I declare that those who can tap into the deep dimensions in the spirit realm through worship will begin to go into the enemy's camp and release the right sound to take back all of the prayers that have been tied up and bound up in Jesus' Name!

<u>Bridge the Gap with Your Sound</u>

It's time to cry loud and spare not; lift up your voice like a trumpet. (Isaiah 58:1a)

Our worship can serve as a medium of sound between our now moments and our miracles!

A *medium* is something such as an intermediate course of action that occupies a position or represents a condition midway between extremes. Let's allow our worship to connect us to our miracles!

<u>Occupy with the Sound</u>

"And he called his ten servants, and delivered them ten pounds, and said unto them, Occupy till I come." Luke 19:13

It's time to occupy your position with your praise and your worship! There are some 24-hour miracles; there are some by-this-time-tomorrow miracles waiting on you, if you would just make a sound! I want to provoke you to release a sound right now! Get mad at the devil, your situation, your financial place in life, and just shout unto God!

Make the devil turn it loose: your new job, your own business, your marriage, your sanity and peace of mind. I charge you now to create a new environment for God to dwell. For some people, all God hears is how much they've been complaining.

Those believers who are able to tap into the right sound in worship will take quantum leaps in the spirit. When you create an atmosphere with the right sound, the mysteries of God are released as well; the spirit of wisdom and revelation unfolds; clarity and illumination starts coming to you about your life and destiny.

When you release the sound, several other things will occur in your life:

1. You will start advancing.
2. An acceleration will take place.
3. You will start acting like who you are supposed to be.
4. Your assignment will be discovered.
5. An aggression will kick in.

Breaking Boundaries

There are boundaries that are created in your soul, and if not detected often, you can find yourself bound up and sometimes not knowing why. It is because you have soul ties to people, places, and certain things or limitations in the mind that have hindered you and held you back.

Some people have soul ties to certain music styles. Even in our services, everyone has their own preferences or perspectives on what and how they think the worship music should be. But you must remember that your emotions are a component within your soul, and if you let them, they will dictate and determine everything about your life, including how you worship God.

These types of ties can block and hinder the flow of God in your time of worship. We are and should be free to worship and praise God with no holds barred, no restrictions, no reservations or drawbacks. We should be free to just go after His presence.

Another part of the soul is the will. We must will ourselves to worship God. You may not feel like it sometimes. Nothing may be going your way, but that's the time when you really need to press in. If you would "will" to open up your mouth and create the sound of worship, it will begin to change your atmosphere.

It is important for you to press your way into His presence because that's when the anointing is going to be released.

People often wonder why they never experience the anointing that accompanies worship. It's because of their inconsistencies in the pursuit of His presence.

You determine the environment you live in. You must make it one of praise and worship.

I just declare right now that whatever soul ties or vices have held you back and away from the presence of God are broken and the curse is being reversed in Jesus' Name. Take your stand, Child of God.

If the presence of God is not in your worship service, it's probably because of a lack of the right sound. Try a new direction in your worship services. Release the youth. Release the prophetic song of the Lord. Worship a litter longer. Praise a little louder. Incorporate anointed drama and dance into the worship service. Release the new sound! God wants to move in your church, but you have to release the right sound—a great sound; a sound that shakes the heavens and affects the earth.

Shift the Sound in Your Home

I've learned to have worship music as well as the Word of God playing in my house. If you are a believer and especially one who leads worship, whether as a choir member, praise team leader, minister, or the like, you must make sure that the sound playing in your house is one that releases God's presence and not the presence of the enemy.

Whoever the secular artists are that are declaring negativity and anything contrary to God's Word in their music are, if their sound is in your house, you must get them out. The words to that music can get in your spirit sublimely and pull you away from the presence of God.

You must bring in the glory! Throw on some great worship from *Jesus Culture*, Eddie James, Freddie Rodriquez, and so on! Do it now if you have to!

Watch the environment in your house change. You are the agent of change for your life. What are you going to do? Don't continue to let the devil in your house. When you open your home up to sounds that have negativity and the anti-Christ spirits associated with them, it's like you are saying,

"You can come on in, devil, and have a seat on the recliner. You want something to drink?"

This is sad, but it's true. What we tend to tolerate we permit! I declare it's time to serve eviction notices to the devil. It's time to give the devil his marching orders.

It is time for our worship teams to shift the atmosphere with sounds from heaven!

It's time to serve papers to all those negative so-called friends. Tell them, "I'm changing my surroundings starting with you!" I hope right now something is beginning to stir in you.

To those of you who are worship leaders, psalmists, and minstrels, because you are an example to those you are leading, you are responsible for the sound you make.

Are you a Psalmist or a Performer?
A Worshipper or a Worrier?
A Shifter or a Settler?

I think some people really don't understand the difference sometimes. As a psalmist, you have the task of creating an atmosphere and causing the heavens to rip open so that the glory can be released in the Earth realm. As a psalmist, you have the ability to change the spiritual climate and make it conducive for miracles to occur. The church is full of Performers; people that have a voice and a talent but have no spiritual sensitivity whatsoever; they're lovers of the attention and the publicity, the lights and media.

The Bible refers to King David as being a man after the heart of God (Acts 13:22). David was in no way a perfect man, but he was a man that stayed before God in worship and had a desire to please Him.

When David found that his city, Ziklag, had been burned down and all the women, children, and possessions had been taken captive, he could have easily given up; especially after all his men turned against him and wanted to stone him. However, he encouraged himself in the Lord (1 Samuel 30:6).

Sometimes in life, your family and friends can be in the same room with you, but because you're in a place they are not, they may not be able to relate or have the words to say that will encourage you. So David chose to make the best out of a bad situation by remembering to worship God.

As a worshipper, you cannot afford to lose the sound that you need to release just because you have had a bad day or things are not going as you expected. You must learn to not let your current condition dictate to your worship life. Remember, we are joint heirs with Christ (Romans 8:17). We are the head and not the tail. We are above and not beneath (Deuteronomy 28).

"Worship is our response, both personal and corporate, to God for who He is, and what He has done; expressed in and by the things we say and the way we live."

~ Louie Giglio ~

True Worship Releases the New Song

"In order for you to move into the new thing, sometimes it is required of us to release the comfort of the old. Sometimes the enemy to new wine is old wine skins. I believe in this hour there's a rising of passionate, holy, consecrated, set apart lovers of Jesus, and uncompromising, who won't settle, but lovers for God that will passionately pursue Him and His kingdom. It's time to shift! Something new is on the horizon."

~ Eddie James ~

"Let the word of Christ dwell in you richly, teaching and exhorting one another with all wisdom, singing psalms, hymns, and spiritual songs, all with grace in your hearts to God." Colossians 3:16 (New English Translation)

"Speaking to yourselves in psalms and hymns and spiritual songs, singing and making melody in your heart to the Lord; Giving thanks always for all things unto God and the Father in the name of our Lord Jesus Christ." Ephesians 5:19–20 (Authorized King James Version)

"And he hath put a new song in my mouth, even praise unto our God: many shall see it, and fear, and shall trust in the LORD." Psalm 40:3

I have learned this truth:

Whenever God is up to something new, a new song is often produced and birthed into the Earth realm.

When I am referring to the new song here, it can be in the form of a tune, melody, and words that have never been sung before or the prophetic song of the Lord that comes like a breath of fresh air to you.

As a worship leader, you must learn to be sensitive to the Spirit of God. The Spirit of God is a progressive spirit. There are things that the Spirit of God wants to release to His people, such as answers about their situations. He wants to reveal to them the seasons that they are in and His heartbeat regarding them.

Worship and praise has a pulse.

Every believer needs to develop the heartbeat of God. Understand that He loves to be worshipped and praised. The Word admonishes us that as we draw near to Him, He will draw near unto us (James 4:8).

I don't know about you, but I need Him as close to me as possible. We sing songs like "Draw Me Close," "More of You," and "Show Us Your Glory," just to name a few, but do we really understand what and who we are singing to?

Prophetic worship, known also as the song of the Lord, is so needed today in our churches. People are in such a place of depravity in the world today. When the prophets and psalmists can minister the song of the Lord over them, it has an explosive power like dynamite that can break them out of their bondages.

I am reminded of my old church, where I learned about the song of the Lord. This ministry had the most significant impact on me as a worshipper. I remember how the ministry gifts would sing a song during their time of ministry, and the results were unbelievable—life-changing even.

One of my first experiences as a recipient of a prophetic song was powerful. I remember my legs could barely hold me up as I felt the presence of God all over me. God spoke right into the intimate areas of my life, and it amazed me. I love that kind of ministry when God uses someone like a worship leader to sing a person out of a prison into a palace. Glory to God! Worship with the new song is necessary if we are going to experience the surprises of God in our lives. There is a place of surprise in our walk with God, but this is only for true worshippers who are open to the new!

The body of Christ has many great men and women of God who flow in the song of the Lord. This is an important aspect to ministry because there are so many hurting people. There are people that have been hurt by each other, by the church, or by a situation in day-to-day life, and they need to experience the love of God that can come through the "new song."

Thank God for some of the forerunners from years ago who first flowed in the song of the Lord; people like Diane Palmer, Mark Chironna, and Tom Bynum. Now, in this time, there are others such as William Mc Dowell, Israel Houghton, Kevin Laver, Eddie James, and *Jesus Culture*. We need this form of worship now like never before!

"I'm writing songs that He might be discovered and not that we be discovered. This has been the greatest freedom for me as a worship leader. Just to be looked through and not at. Worship is more than a monologue. It's a dialogue; it's a conversation with you and God. Worship is not a time-filler!"

~ Israel Houghton ~

<u>Chamber of Worship Scripture Library</u>

I believe that the following scriptures are definitely passages that worship leaders should have a knowledge and understanding of:

Psalm 29:2 – "Ascribe to the LORD the glory due his name; worship the LORD in the splendor of holiness." (ESV)

Psalm 66:4 – "All the earth worships you and sings praises to you; they sing praises to your name. Selah." (ESV)

Psalm 95:6 – "Oh come, let us worship and bow down; let us kneel before the LORD, our Maker!" (ESV)

Psalm 99:5 – "Exalt ye the LORD our God, and worship at his footstool; for he is holy."Romans 12:1–2 – "I appeal to you therefore, brothers, by the mercies of God, to present your bodies as a living sacrifice, holy and acceptable to God, which is your spiritual worship. Do not be conformed to this world, but be transformed by the renewal of your mind, that by testing you may discern what is the will of God, what is good and acceptable and perfect." (ESV)

John 4:21–24 – "Jesus said to her, 'Woman, believe me, the hour is coming when neither on this mountain nor in Jerusalem will you worship the Father. You worship what you do not know; we worship what we know, for salvation is from the Jews. But the hour is coming, and is now here, when the true worshipers will worship the Father in spirit and truth, for the Father is seeking such people to worship him. God is spirit, and those who worship him must worship in spirit and truth.'" (ESV)

Revelation 4:11 – "Worthy are you, our Lord and God, to receive glory and honor and power, for you created all things, and by your will they existed and were created." (ESV)

"To worship is to quicken the conscience by the holiness of God, to feed the mind with the truth of God, to purge the imagination by the beauty of God, to open the heart to the love of God, to devote the will to the purpose of God."

~ William Temple ~

True Worship Releases the Gifts to Flow

"One of the most powerful things about worship, prayer, and spending time with God is this: Worship gives us access; it is a portal to God! So through the vehicle of worship we've gained unprecedented access to the presence of God where the secrets of heaven are revealed and when declared will change things on the earth."

~ William McDowell ~

I must reiterate something said in another chapter regarding sound. There is always a sound that precedes a move of God. Wherever you hear of and see in history great moves of the spirit, it can be traced back to a sound that causes the gifts to flow.

Elisha called for the minstrel to play, and the spirit of prophesy fell on him and he began to prophesy. 2 Kings 3:15

The Hebrew word *minstrel* in 2 Kings 3:15 properly signifies a player upon a stringed instrument like the harp. David played this instrument before Saul.

"Let our lord now command thy servants, which are before thee, to seek out a man, who is a cunning player on an harp: and it shall come to pass, when the evil spirit from God is upon thee, that he shall play with his hand, and thou shalt be well." 1 Samuel 16:16

"And it came to pass on the morrow, that the evil spirit from God came upon Saul, and he prophesied in the midst of the house: and David played with his hand, as at other times: and there was a javelin in Saul's hand." 1 Samuel 18:10

"And the evil spirit from the LORD was upon Saul, as he sat in his house with his javelin in his hand: and David played with his hand." 1 Samuel 19:9

Praise & Worship Opens Spiritual Doors

We need the operation of the gifts in our churches today. Praise and Worship provides a breeding ground for the nine gifts of the Spirit to operate and function.

"And there are differences of administrations, but the same Lord. And there are diversities of operations, but it is the same God which worketh all in all. But the manifestation of the Spirit is given to every man to profit withal. For to one is given by the Spirit the word of wisdom; to another the word of knowledge by the same Spirit; To another faith by the same Spirit; to another the gifts of healing by the same Spirit; To another the working of miracles; to another prophecy; to another discerning of spirits; to another divers kinds of tongues; to another the interpretation of tongues: But all these worketh that one and the selfsame Spirit, dividing to every man severally as he will." 1 Corinthians 12:5–11

Paul penned this letter on the gifts of the Spirit in the New Testament to provide insight of their relevancy to the Church. There is no legitimate excuse for the gifts not flowing in our worship services. God intends for all people—your family, your friends, your co-workers, your neighbors, even your enemies—to be reached. Everything and everyone in the body of Christ has a part to play in this happening.

We must learn to be sensitive to the move of the Spirit. There was a song I remember singing years ago that says, "When the Lord gets ready, you got to move." I think for some of us we have a proclivity to not understand the meaning of the songs we sing because many of the people that sang songs like that did not move anywhere.

Sometimes our lives totally contradict the songs that we sing. God has a plan for the gifts to operate in our churches. There are diversities of gifts for the purpose of building up and strengthening our churches. Paul further explained that there are nine specific gifts, but they are all of the same Spirit.

The gifts are not for the people that have them. God intends for others to be ministered to through the grace and gift He places on you. The sad thing is there are churches that preach and speak against the gifts of the Spirit and to some extent become barren and dry people. Their callings wither away, and many die of spiritual malnutrition. Some even miscarry in the Spirit.

What a sad moment in history when the church shuts the spiritual doors to God moving in our praise and worship services. These ministries become cold and insensitive. They become average or, worse, below average churches. God has not called us to be average. To be average is like being an enemy to God. He wants you to walk in your calling. He wants you to bless others and change lives with the gifts He's given you.

I remember in a season of my life where I was literally withering away. The gifting that God, not man, had bestowed upon me was drying up.

I had to take that situation to God and get His direction. We must always know He has a plan and a place for us. At that time, I knew this but would not move on it until there was a release. I totally believe in doing things in order. Of course, I went to my man of God and expressed my concerns, and the rest, in a nut shell, is history. Here I am today. I totally can relate to people that are in dry places in life; in your spirit and in your church. God has a solution.

If He did it for me, He can do it for you. He led me to a place, and like a man that's been in a desert for years, moisture came and I found my oasis. We all at some point in life, if we keep it moving, will discover our oasis in a desert land. Praise God!

"The steps of a good man are ordered by the LORD: and he delighteth in his way." Psalm 37:23

Don't Taint the Gifts

There tends to be a lack of revelation regarding the gifts of the Spirit. When people don't understand something, they criticize it. Then, on the other hand, with so much going on now with people misusing their gifts, God is saying I won't have any part in sin.

Remember the story of the Prophet Eli? He had two sons: Hophni and Phinehas. They did everything and anything that they wanted to do. It was ignored by Eli, but finally God said enough is enough.

As a result of Eli ignoring the sin that was going on, it opened up the door for the presence of the Lord to eventually depart the temple. The place they were in became known as Ichabod, which is to imply the glory of the Lord has departed from this place. I don't know about you, child of God, but I cannot live without His presence. I can't breathe without His presence. He is and always has been so good and real to me. So I encourage you today, worship leader, pastor, song writer, stay in the rhythm of God. Get His heartbeat. Allow yourself to learn how to wait in His presence.

"But they that wait upon the LORD shall renew their strength; they shall mount up with wings as eagles; they shall run, and not be weary; and they shall walk, and not faint." Isaiah 40:31

Waiting, in this scripture, implies patience and hope. The word wait here in the Hebrew is *qavah,* which means to expect, to look for.

While waiting in His presence, expect for God to move and do something, to reveal Himself and show Himself strong. Look for the gifts to operate and bring breakthrough where other administrations cannot. Allow the gifts to manifest and flow. It will be like a breath of fresh air.

I hear the Lord saying: The time is over for my people continuing to be suffocated. You have had no fresh air, but now the time has come for you to live, to know who I really am says the Lord. For I am releasing rain and oil from my throne even now, and those that will receive—your lives will be changed. The winds are starting to blow again says the Lord. Just jump in; take the plunge, for I am there to take you to the place in me, a place of moisture, a place where I am revealed says the Lord. Get ready for rain!

"The time has come for a revival of public worship as the finest of the fine arts.... While there is a call for strong preaching there is even a greater need for uplifting worship."
~Andrew W. Blackwood ~

I love what happens in a place when the Spirit of God falls like a blanket in it. Just to see lives impacted, infused, and influenced by the anointing is amazing.

"Behold, I will do a new thing; now it shall spring forth; shall ye not know it? I will even make a way in the wilderness, and rivers in the desert." Isaiah 43:19

Some of our churches don't operate in the gifts because they simply choose not to. Others lack revelation on the subject. Some of us have been in services where we have seen the hand of God move. Then, on the other hand, some have been in services where the potential for God to move was there. However, the presence of the Lord was ignored!

People today in the church need more than religion. They need a God encounter. The world is in such a place where people are under attack, pressured, stressed out, depressed, and oppressed of the devil.

So immediately what this conveys to me is that we need the presence of the Lord to infiltrate our church services. People's lives and destinies have the potential to be aborted when we ignore what God often wants to do in praise and worship.

"It's imperative that we never reserve our worship, because when we don't exalt Him we lessen the impact of His presence on the earth. No one is saved or drawn to Him."

~ Pastor Clint Brown ~

I believe that when worship is prevalent, it produces power, which reveals purpose. Worship in our churches serves more than for the purpose of having music playing in the atmosphere. There is a portal that is opened by way of the heavens, and the Spirit of God begins to manifest in various forms.

Destroying the Yokes

We have been taught that according to Scripture, it's the anointing that destroys the yoke (Isaiah 10:27). This is true. However, in order for yokes to be destroyed, you have to be able to identify them to deal with them. Worship begins to reveal the yokes that need to be destroyed. Understand that there is a difference between the presence of God and the anointing of God. The anointing is only introduced to us after we've pressed through to His presence. They both work hand in hand. You cannot bypass His presence to get to the anointing for yokes to be destroyed.

I taught an extensive series once on the "Authentic Anointing" versus the "Counterfeit Anointing." A counterfeit anointing feels like God and sounds like God, but when it comes time to produce, it can't perform the task at hand. Look at the seven sons of Sceva in the book of Acts, chapter 19. Remember what the evil spirit asked them: "Jesus I know, Paul I know, but who are you?"

We are in a culture where there are those who just go all out for God's presence while others are more seeker-friendly, reserved, and laid back. They are those who just don't think "all of that" is necessary. Needless to say, everyone has an opinion about the gifts flowing in full operation. I understand there are people that may visit your services, and you don't want to scare them off. However, I know that when it comes down to His presence or you, I will choose Him!

In many ways, the world is getting more "spiritual" and being bold about its faith and beliefs regarding spiritual matters. However, in many ways, the church is in a state where it is on spiritual life support. It's almost like it is gradually dying in some areas. We need the spiritual defibrillator of worship and the gifts to bring back to life that which is dying. So let it be in Jesus' Name!

Key Holders with the Key of David

"And the key of the house of David will I lay upon his shoulder; so he shall open, and none shall shut; and he shall shut, and none shall open." Isaiah 22:22

"And to the angel of the church in Philadelphia write; These things saith he that is holy, he that is true, he that hath the key of David, he that openeth, and no man shutteth; and shutteth, and no man openeth;" Revelation 3:7

There is what I want to call *key holders* in the body of Christ. Likened unto King David, they will have the ability to pull sounds and notes from out of heaven to shift and charge the atmosphere for the gifts to function. They have their ears constantly by the mouth of God. As He speaks, they release it in the Earth realm through song.

We need more key holders in our worship services today. Some of the key holders of today are people like Jason Upton, Eddie James, Kim Walker, Israel Houghton, David Binion, and Trent Cory, just to name a few. Please forgive me if I didn't mention your name. Your gift is just as important to the body of Christ as well. We need you all.

The key holders possess something that the average singer and musician do not have. They are able to assist in creating moments in the Holy Ghost.

We all know that with a key in the natural it serves the purpose of granting us access to something on the other side. In the simplest form, we understand that a key unlocks doors. Ironically here, how often have we lost our keys in the natural? It can be frustrating, especially when you know you just had them. Now the question is, where did I last see them?

In some of our churches, we have lost our keys, the keys to worship and praise. The keys have been misplaced. But I declare that they must be found for access in other dimensions in the spirit. There are heights and depths in the spirit that we can go when there's a key holder in the house.

We need the five-fold ministry gifts using their gifts in full operation in the body of Christ.

"And he gave some, apostles; and some, prophets; and some, evangelists; and some, pastors and teachers;" Ephesians 4:11

These gifts and operations need the grace and the anointing of worship to assist in breaking through the rough places; the tight spots in our services; the dry patches!

Many times it has been documented in history that lives and nations were changed because of the gifts operating. There are nations that have received prophetic words that altered the course of history. Maybe you, too, can attest to the fact that had it not been for the gifts in operation, your life possibly wouldn't have been impacted as much.

I know so many can testify of the goodness of the Lord portrayed through the gifts working. I can't begin to count the times where I received a prophetic word or even witnessed the gifts in operation. It's mind blowing.

I've been in services where I've seen for myself healings take place; the working of miracles; words of wisdom and knowledge. As a prophet myself, I have ministered to people who were on the verge of suicide, but the prophetic word aborted the plan of the devil. Glory to God!

The devil knows the power that lies in the gifts flowing. He knows that it can help to build your faith as well. So the enemy will try and cause religion and tradition to stifle and block the gifts from flowing. If you place lids on the gifts, it's like being in a plastic bag with no air. You'll die and wither away with no *zoe* (Greek word for life) of God! But when it's removed, fresh air comes!

Freedom in the Holy Ghost is what we need in our churches. I declare a shift in your services right now in Jesus' Name! I declare the mantle of Climate Changers begins to emerge! Pastors remember this: It's not your church! It never was. It has and always will belong to God! You have stewardship privileges.

I even declare that the spirit of Saul and Pharaoh be broken in Jesus' Name!

"Now the Lord is that Spirit: and where the Spirit of the Lord is, there is liberty. But we all, with open face beholding as in a glass the glory of the Lord, are changed into the same image from glory to glory, even as by the Spirit of the Lord." 2 Corinthians 3:17–18

"Don't let life affect your worship; let your worship affect life."

~ LaMar Boschman ~

You Cannot Allow Jezebel to Rule Worship

"The spirit of Jezebel and the House of Ahab are ruling and reigning supreme in culture, government, media, and even the church to some extent. I believe God's answer is not just to release the prophets and those in 'full-time ministry' to take care of the problem. His longing is to activate and anoint everyday kings in their place of authority to rise up and take a stand against injustice, perversion, and unrighteousness, and every high place must come down."

~ Sean Feucht ~

Jezebel is in the form of anything that is not the authentic presence of God. Even though Jezebel is a part of biblical history, the spirit she operated in is still very much alive in the world today. It carries a gold-plated anointing and poses as the real thing when, in fact, it is not pure gold. It has a form of godliness but denies the power thereof.

Here's some insight into the character and spirit of Jezebel as noted at gotquestions.org, "What Is the Spirit of Jezebel?":

> "Jezebel's story is found in 1 and 2 Kings. She was the daughter of Ethbaal, king of Tyre/Sidon and priest of the cult of Baal, a cruel, sensuous and revolting false god whose worship involved sexual degradation and lewdness. Ahab, king of Israel, married Jezebel and led the nation into Baal worship

(1 Kings 16:31). Ahab and Jezebel's reign over Israel is one of the saddest stories in the history of God's people.

There are two incidents in the life of Jezebel which characterize her and may define what is meant by the Jezebel spirit.

One trait is her obsessive passion for domineering and controlling others, especially in the spiritual realm. When she became queen, she began a relentless campaign to rid Israel of all evidences of Jehovah worship. She ordered the extermination of all the prophets of the Lord (1 Kings 18:4, 13) and replaced their altars with those of Baal. Her strongest enemy was Elijah, who demanded a contest on Mount Carmel between the powers of Israel's God and the powers of Jezebel and the priests of Baal (1 Kings 18).

Of course, Jehovah won, but despite hearing of the miraculous powers of Jehovah, Jezebel refused to repent and swore on her gods that she would pursue Elijah relentlessly and take his life.

Her stubborn refusal to see and submit to the power of the living God would lead her to a hideous end. 2 Kings 9:29-37

The second incident involves a righteous man named Naboth who refused to sell to Ahab land adjoining the palace, rightly declaring that to sell his inheritance would be against the Lord's command. 1 Kings 21:3; Leviticus 25:23

While Ahab sulked and fumed on his bed, Jezebel taunted and ridiculed him for his weakness, then proceeded to have the innocent Naboth framed and stoned to death.

Naboth's sons were also stoned to death, so there would be no heirs, and the land would revert to the possession of the king.

Such a single-minded determination to have one's way, no matter who is destroyed in the process, is a characteristic of the Jezebel spirit.

So infamous was Jezebel's sexual immorality and idol worship that the Lord Jesus Himself refers to her in a warning to the church at Thyatira (Revelation 2:18–29).

Most likely referring to a woman in the church who influenced it the same way Jezebel influenced Israel into idolatry and sexual immorality, Jesus declares to the Thyatirans that she is not to be tolerated. Whoever this woman was, like Jezebel, she refused to repent of her immorality and her false teaching, and her fate was sealed. The Lord Jesus cast her onto a sick bed, along with those who committed idolatry with her.

The end for those who succumb to a Jezebel spirit is always death and destruction, both in the physical and the spiritual sense.

Perhaps the best way to define the Jezebel spirit is to say it characterizes anyone who acts in the same manner as Jezebel did, engaging in immorality, idolatry (making something more important than God), false teaching and unrepentant sin.

To go beyond that is to engage in conjecture and can possibly lead to false accusations and divisiveness within the body of Christ." (Gotquestions.org, "What Is the Spirit of Jezebel?")

If you read 1 Kings 18, it will give more insight into Jezebel's evil influence over the worship in Israel. Proverbs 16:25 says that "There is a way that seemeth right unto man, but the end thereof are the ways of death."

Characteristics of the Jezebel Spirit

Keep in mind that spirits do not have a gender, so this spirit can be found in both males and females. Some characteristics of the Jezebel spirit include:

1. They are very competitive and love to win the influence, status, and advantage over others.
2. They are often never wrong.
3. They manage to get in places of authority and are often difficult to remove once they are in.
4. They have sociopathic characteristics.

5. They gain power by eliminating others from the equation, especially their opponents.

6. They are controlling and bossy.

7. They are manipulative and are good at influencing with gifts, words, flattery, sexual advances, or any other form of temptation that appeals to the flesh.

8. They tend to be backbiters and whisperers as referred to in Romans 1:29–30. They work behind the scenes recruiting others against their victims, especially those who have any type of leadership or status qualities.

9. They are very persuasive and like to recruit others. They do not give up until their recruits are won over. If the potential recruits don't cooperate, this angers and frustrates them.

10. They love to help but only with the secret intention of gaining influence for their own selfish reasons.

11. They can be narcissistic.

12. They can be overly sensitive, especially to correction.

13. They tend to play the role of victim themselves in order to gain sympathy.

14. Being the center of attention really pleases them even if they pretend it does not.

15. They fail at conforming to the regular rules and established standards set forth.

16. They always have a compelling and often convincing excuse when they are wrong.

17. They will isolate themselves from the group, especially if they feel they can't be the one controlling things either openly or behind the scenes.

18. They often have a problem with submitting to the set order in place.

These are just some of the main behavior patterns to make you aware as you are placing individuals in an authoritative position on your worship team.

Based on the above criteria, if you find that someone on your worship team already qualifies and is operating under the spirit of Jezebel, there are some things that you can do. Be encouraged and know that for everything the devil can throw at you, if God is for you, who can be against you? God always has a way out and a solution to any problem.

Since these individuals usually have achieved some level of authority, only someone who has more authority than they do or a group effort will work. If you are a woman leader and you need to confront this spirit, you must be strong and self-confident.

If you are a man, you need to be the same, but make sure you will not allow yourself to be manipulated by looks and tears if it is a woman that has this spirit. If it is a man that has the spirit, don't be moved or concerned by threats. However, I do encourage you that if at any time you have observed violent hostility from the person, in this day and age you should have back up; not just spiritual but physical.

<u>Confronting Jezebel</u>

Depending on the situation, it might even be necessary to have church security or some type of law enforcement involved if they are a potential threat. Here are some other guidelines to help you when confronting this spirit:

1. Make sure you are not an enabler or an "Ahab" yourself.
2. Address the behavior by pointing out facts, and make sure you have proof. Do not start by accusing them of having this spirit. You will get nowhere because their defenses will be up and their excuses will be compelling. It is key that you ask a lot of questions, especially regarding why they behave the way they do and do some of the things that they do.
3. Be prepared with your list of concerns and have proof.
4. Gather witnesses that are credible, faithful believers as well; those who are in leadership positions work best.
5. Deal with them alone, not with their posse. This makes them more vulnerable and removes the source of their power, which is the influence they have over others.
6. Minister to them on the subject of repentance.
7. If they do repent or show a willingness to change, then minister deliverance to them. Cast out the spirit in Jesus' Name. Keep a record of this incident and warn them against being controlled by this spirit in the future. Also, minister to them the importance of having a renewed mind. If they do not change their belief system, their behavior will revert back to being influenced by this spirit. Once the spirit is gone, the person needs support and counseling to examine how

the spirit entered to begin with so they can close the door on further attempts by the spirit to enter.

8. Reject them if they decide not to repent. Cut off ties with them, telling them forgiveness and deliverance is always available to them.

Spiritual Warfare

Spiritual warfare, in short, is the spiritual fight of good versus evil. It is the warfare that is taking place between angels and demons; the church and the world's system; and the inner struggle of believers against the lusts of the flesh.

"For the weapons of our warfare are not carnal, but mighty through God to the pulling down of strong holds;" 2 Corinthians 10:4

In this mission to rid Jezebel or any other spirit contrary to the spirit of God, you must implement spiritual warfare, which happens to be another dimension of praise and worship. When you enter into high dimensions of praise and worship, oftentimes you will shift into what I call a worshipping warrior mode.

This might require necessary travailing; decreeing and declaring. In some battles, you have to learn to get all the way down in the spiritual trenches so that you can take back what has been taken from you.

"And from the days of John the Baptist until now the kingdom of heaven suffereth violence, and the violent take it by force." Matthew 11:12

Know this, that your warfare is determined by what you are carrying. So my question to you, child of destiny, is, "Do you know what you are carrying?" Selah!

Remember as you are warring and worshipping that you must rely on God's power, not your own. You must war covered with the blood of Jesus and going in the name of Jesus and not your own.

Put on the Whole Armor

Make sure you have on the full armor of God as outlined in Ephesians 6. It is so important when going to war that you take an assessment check. Every good soldier checks his or her gear to make sure it is good. As believers, we must make sure that when waging war, we are armed entirely with the armor of God. Finally, remember that we always fight the enemy with the Word of God. (Matthew 4:4)

To be effective, you must arm yourself with the entire armor of God. Some believers today only have certain parts. Some have the helmets. Some have the breastplates. Some have the shield of faith. In other words, they pick the parts that they think work for them. It's like this in most of our churches; some want worship and praise while others want testimony service. All some want is choir music and some just the hymns.

The reality is we need all of God that we can get, but we must go after Him. Some churches want prophesy. Some say it doesn't take all of that. It's almost like we can get stuck in a time zone. Everything stays the same, and you think that you'll be okay. No you won't! Revelation is the key. When it is true revelation, you must be able to see it for yourself. Even we see in Peter's encounter with Jesus how important revelation is.

"And Jesus answered and said unto him, Blessed art thou, Simon Barjona: for flesh and blood hath not revealed it unto thee, but my Father which is in heaven." Matthew 16:17

If the devil can hijack your worship service, he will.

If you have ever been in a place where there was much resistance or where it was so hard to break through in worship, it's because there is warfare going on. It can feel like there are people intentionally coming to church to quench the Spirit of God.

Even if this is the case, you must remember it is a spirit that you are dealing with, and most people come into the house of God to not only hear the word but to have a worship experience as well. I often say to our people:

"Don't ever give a person power over your praise!"

That's too much authority to give to someone. The time is up for coming in bound and leaving out bound. There are spirits that come and sit on individuals you may sit next to, and you'll find yourself holding back on your praise.

The spirit of Jezebel not only has an assignment to kill the prophets but to dry up the worship part of our services and to quench the anointing of God in the place. Understand that when the right atmosphere is created, the prophetic shortly follows. Streams of revelation are imparted into God's people about what they may be going through. Many receive clarity about their situation and even their purpose.

I have found out personally that as I began to go deeper in worship, God began to unfold His will and plans for my life. Things started becoming clearer and clearer.

Worship in your life will do what a lens will do for a camera when it's adjusted right. It will bring you focus.

In many churches when the worship service begins to go deeper, someone will cut it off because things begin to get too unfamiliar. This is the reason why there is such a lack of "moisture" in the atmosphere. Now understand, I'm not talking about allowing the worship service to get spooky and crazy as previously mentioned in another chapter, but I'm talking about allowing the authentic breakthrough to come in. Sometimes this may mean people are getting really emotional to the point they are weeping and crying and deliverance is taking place.

Just don't let the spirit of Jezebel operate and control the atmosphere of the service, stifling the breakthrough that is coming. I will call it what it is, even though it may be as a result of lack of information on the subject of praise and worship for some. The other side to this is witchcraft; a form of control during the worship experience when breakthrough starts help among the congregation and the worship is cut off by those leading.

While I'm on the subject here also, pastor and leaders not wanting their members to fellowship with other ministries can become a form of mind control, which is associated with Jezebel. Oftentimes it is good for members to get out and see what other ministries are doing, especially in the area of worship. Think of it like this: "It's good to go out to dinner every once and while to eat instead of just always eating at home."

You must remember they are not your sheep. They belong to God! God allows you the opportunity to cover them! You work for Him. It's not the other way around. Our churches need to be free from Jezebel and any other opposing force that hinders us from the presence of God. Our churches need the rain and oil of heaven to fall every time.

<u>Don't Sit on the Worship!</u>

We never know what someone may be going through or dealing with. The power of praise and worship can break the neck of the devil, oppression, sickness, depression, discouragement, and negative thinking. It's a key that unlocks many doors! Praise God!

Most of our churches today have the dynamics of the word but lack the dynamics of life-changing worship and praise. I've seen it time and time again where pastors and leaders, because they have a sermon to preach or an "itch" to preach, have literally sat on the worship experience that was about to break out.

Get over it! God at times will deliver His people through praise and worship. We need more pastors and leaders today that are not controlling and dominating the services but instead are making themselves available and sensitive to the move of God for however and whenever God wants to move. We must remember that the spirit of Jezebel may not always be working in the congregants. Sometimes it's through the leadership.

<u>Throw Jezebel from the Tower</u>

"And Jehu the son of Nimshi shalt thou anoint to be king over Israel: and Elisha the son of Shaphat of Abelmeholah shalt thou anoint to be prophet in thy room." 1 Kings 19:16

Lord, release your sons and daughters of Jehu! The Bible talks of this man called Jehu playing a vital part in the assassination of Jezebel. He was known as a king of Israel especially noted for his furious chariot attacks.

His name not only means "Jehovah is he," but I love this part: "a skilled driver, one who is fast." This makes me think of the movie *Fast and Furious* with all the skilled drivers. Jehu was fast and furious, and because of that, he was able to take out the spirit of Jezebel.

Someone with a spirit like Jehu is who you need to take down the spirit of Jezebel; someone who is going to be swift and not play with the devil; someone who knows what they are doing. God let this anointing increase on those who You have appointed to do so!

The author of 1 Kings says that Jehu entered the city without resistance. He saw Jehoram's mother, Jezebel, watching him with contempt from a palace window. He then commanded the palace eunuchs to throw her from the window. This is symbolic of removing her from her high place and breaking the spell and control that she had.

When Jezebel is thrown from the tower, you become free. You are free to operate according to the plans that God has for you which are good (Jeremiah 29:11). You must know that God never intended for you to be bound up in religion or inside of a box. *I declare unto you that the time is now to awaken from your place of slumber.* Begin to lift your hands right where you are and go after God.

Jezebel was killed, and Jehu drove his chariot over her body. Off the tower she went and down to the ground she fell. When her servants came later to bury her, they found that dogs had eaten all but her hands, feet, and skull. We need an impartation of the Jehu Anointing today in our churches that will destroy that spirit in its entirety.

Again, the Bible declared that Jehu drove furiously. He was focused on his objective, which was to get Jezebel off that high place and have her destroyed. Jezebel doesn't belong on top of our services. She's been in many of the churches for too long. So God will raise up someone who is not intimidated by religion and tradition; someone willing to go against the grain. We need Jehus in the body of Christ today who can take back the authority in worship.

I encourage you to read the story of Jehu, and you'll notice how even at one point he left the door open when he went in to take care of Jezebel. This was as if to say, "This isn't going to take long. I'm not about to waste your time or my time." Remember, too, that Jehu was the same prophet of God that gathered hundreds of Baal worshippers together and killed them. (2 Kings 10)

In summary, the best way you can wage warfare against this spirit operating in your worship services is to remember and practice these four things:

1. Always rely on God's power and not any person's natural ability or talent.
2. Remember that only what you do for Christ will last. So keep that as your motivation for all the decisions that you make and all that you do.
3. Protect yourself by walking in the Word. The only way you can do this is by staying in it.
4. Do not tolerate Jezebel. Do not allow her to control your worship services any longer! Throw her off the tower!

"We throw around the word intimacy a lot. Oh, I'm intimate with the Lord! It's impossible to be intimate with your clothes on with God. He strips away everything, and when He gets finished with you, there's nothing."

~ Lindell Cooley ~

It Takes Time to Build an Effective Worship Ministry

"Worship leaders, don't try to engage the crowd; instead lead the crowd to join you in engaging God."

~ Pastor Steven Furtick ~

Expert author David Good states in "Keys to Building a Healthy Worship Ministry" (ezinearticles.com):

"One of our top priorities as leaders should be to not only build a great sounding and musically proficient worship team, but an overall healthy one. It doesn't matter if you are starting from scratch, have inherited an existing program, are big or small. You can develop a healthy music ministry. Raise the bar in your music department and watch your team rise up to meet the challenge."

Way too often, some ministries don't take the proper time to build effective worship ministries because they feel that they don't have the time or they just don't have the energy. One of my spiritual mothers in the faith, Dr. Bridget Hilliard, says:

"An excuse is the crutch for the uncommitted."

If you are committed to worshipping God, then you should be committed to seeing others come into His presence through praise and worship. There are some nuts and bolts that you need to utilize in order to establish an effective worship ministry. Always remember that it's never about you; it's about God!

"Let all things be done decently and in order." 1 Corinthians 14:40

Establish Your Worship Style

Well of course one of the most obvious things when it comes to building a worship ministry is establishing your style of worship. You must have a desire to have this area of your worship arts ministry expand and enlarge. Your style will be based upon the median age group of your church. As you examine this, it will assist you in getting a gage for the type of worship style that works for you.

Everyone does not worship the same way. However, all of our objectives should be to glorify the Father. A lack of cohesiveness and focus is one of the greatest challenges for worship leaders and teams.

Start Where You Are

When starting a worship team or ministry, it's important to start where you're at. If you don't have all the perks you see other churches do, don't be discouraged. Your day will come when you will have an entire praise band and team of worship leaders.

I remember when we started our team of worship leaders. It was a tedious and difficult process. We started out with CDs. It was very difficult to attempt to try and flow with a CD. I know for some that sounds familiar, right? Needless to say, we used what we had, and besides the occasional skip every now and then, it worked out fine.

As time passed, we began to evolve and did not need the CDs. It has been a process, and we are learning, growing, and getting better every week. The good thing is there is change that I can identify. After going through a dozen or more musicians and several worship leaders, things have finally started to fall into place. We have established a faithful core of worship leaders that is growing daily to the glory of God. There were times, of course, when I didn't know how things would turn out. But the current team has remained faithful and stayed the course.

Presently, we are experiencing high moments of praise and very intimate moments of worship. Just to see this come to fruition is priceless. We have formed a worship movement called *Generation N-Ter-N*, a group of young people giving their gifts to the Lord through praise and worship.

Maybe you have been frustrated and discouraged, wondering, "When, Lord, and how?" Let me just encourage you worship leader, worship pastor. One of my favorite scriptures in the word is "For I know the thoughts that I think toward you, saith the LORD, thoughts of peace, and not of evil, to give you an expected end (Jeremiah 29:11)." Just hold on and stay the course, and you will see God's plans unfold for you.

Team Members Must Be Married to the Vision

The ones that you select to be a part of the worship ministry must be married to the vision of the house. Just like Joshua was connected to Moses despite the tests and attacks that came from others among the nation, you need people that you, too, can count on. They need to be faithful to the ministry and support it financially as well as prayerfully.

Every worship ministry must have a worship team or pastor that is submitted to the vision of the house. There is no "You can come on in and take over the show." No! There's a working together to complete the task of a well-rounded ministry. Often in this area, people come with their own agendas of sorts. They would rather be seen or heard or have the chance of controlling the service.

It's so important that whomever the set man or woman of God appoints as the worship leader has a lifestyle that is in accordance with the Word of God. There's no double agent here; no down low in the closet thing going on here. You're either 100 percent all in or not. In other words, there is no room for doing your own thing.

They have to be someone that has been proven and tried. They must be someone who is born again and living a holy life; not someone that can just carry a note.

Here's more valuable information that can help you in your selection process:

> "8 Steps to Developing a Healthy Team" by David Good:

> #1 – Have a biblically sound purpose for what you are doing. I have found that nothing develops commitment better than giving people a clear sense of

purpose. Put the vision for the worship team in writing and talk about it often with them.

#2 – Choose your team carefully. Don't make musical talent or ability the only criteria for choosing members of your team. I have a mantra:

"Any drummer is not better than no drummer."

It is vital that you have auditions and personal interviews for anyone who wants to join the worship team. This will help prevent problems before they arise.

#3 – Develop a "team" mentality with your group. Don't allow any hint of a "diva" spirit to have a place on your team. It will kill it. Tell your team often that everyone is important and needed. Use words like "us" and avoid words like "I" or "me."

#4 – Build people, not a program. People want to know that you genuinely care about them, not just what they can do for you. Their well being must always be more important than what you can get out of them. People that know you truly care for them will be there for you.

#5 – Know where you are going. If you don't have a sense of direction, people won't follow you. This doesn't mean you have all the answers and have it all figured out. It means that you have spent time seeking God for direction and are trying to follow Him. This builds trust and trust builds commitment. If your team knows that you are being led by the Holy Spirit, they will trust you.

#6 – Be a shepherd, not just a director. In other words, you need to not only lead them musically but spiritually. Make sure your rehearsals aren't just about practicing music but building character. Visit them in the hospital. Call (or text) them when they miss a rehearsal.

#7 – Let others lead alongside you. Encourage and develop leaders in your team. Perhaps someone is better at arranging or rehearsing vocals. Let them do it for you. Remember, you can't do it alone.

#8 – Let God be in control at all times. If you let Him lead you, you'll be amazed at how much easier and more enjoyable ministry will be.

How about instead of trying to get God to bless what we are doing, we find out what God is already blessing and do that? Easier said than done, I know, but it takes all the pressure off of us to make things happen. Learn to follow Him and let Him make it all happen.

May the Lord bless you and your team with health and vitality.

David Good, http://newsongsofpraise.blogspot.com, Article Source: http://EzineArticles.com/?expert=David_Good, Article Source: http://EzineArticles.com/3603797

<u>Paid Worship Leaders</u>

I personally am all for this! However, there should be a "protocol for the prospect." If you are a church seeking a paid worship leader, you must inspect what you expect.

For those ministries that are looking for a worship leader, remember that everyone must be proven!

We have so much trouble in this area because people tend to get desperate for a great worship leader. You just can't let a pretty voice come in and lead your people.

Vision is very important. If you desire to take on the role in a church as a paid worship leader, one of the first things that I would strongly suggest that you inquire about is the vision of the church and the worship team. Find out the heartbeat of that house. This means, for the most part, what the senior pastor wants for the ministry. It's not what you want. The first rule is:

It's always about kingdom order.

There has been so much prostitution in the church: pimping prophets, whoring worship leaders, manipulative minstrels, and performing psalmists. It's almost to the point where certain churches don't want the praise and worship experience. It's been abused and misused so much. But I declare God is raising up worship leaders that have His heart, mind, and spirit.

The Worship Rehearsals

There has to be a change and a charge in the area of your worship leading. Order is a must; even in your praise rehearsals. You just can't throw a group of people together and, because they're talented or prophetic, expect them to flow. There has to be a grooming time, a uniting time, and a time of learning the flow of each other.

There needs to be a time when the praise team along with the worship pastor and minstrels get together and pray together. There needs to be periodic worship sessions where you're just flowing together for at least 10–15 minutes. There also should be a time set aside for just the band to gel and practice together. It takes time for a unit to develop. All of you working together are a work in progress.

You must keep in mind also that everyone's level of worship is not the same. Let's just be real here. Some have to come higher and get with the program, otherwise they can't be a part. If they can't commit, they must get off the team. You must understand that a lot of people are for show. However, the true worshippers are there to grow. Throw the Jonahs off the boat!

Transitioning and Flowing Between Songs

I have found that this is a key area in maintaining spiritual cohesiveness and keeping the flow of the worship service. In formal church settings, where the service is often with hymn books, there is probably no need to consider how to transition between songs. However, in contemporary settings, due to our "free style" of worship, this is not the case. While musicians may be comfortable playing through song arrangements that have been rehearsed, they may be uncertain about how to link songs and maintain a sense of "flow" through the worship time.

Having an awkward gap at the end of a song while the minstrels try and bring in the next song can be a real distraction for the congregation, especially if they were deeply engaged in the worship. So here are a few tips to help with the flow of the worship songs:

1. Fine tune your introductions and closings to your songs. Make sure you rehearse these parts especially because this is usually a time when the congregation isn't singing and will notice any uncertainty on your part.

2. When you are closing out a fast song, end it big. Have the minstrels hold a big final chord or play a few extra bars before stopping. Then immediately have your drummer count in the next song to ensure it comes in at the right pace. It is important to make sure that you keep this gap short.

3. When moving between slower songs, it is important to maintain continuity. Don't let them stop playing at the end of the song. Instead, have the keyboard player hold the tonic chord.

4. If your next song is in the same key, it will be easy to make a transition without a gap. However, ensure you are working at the new tempo before starting the song if it is different (or at least start decisively at the new tempo). If the new song is in a different key, then try playing the repeating sequence right up to the point where the new song needs to start, then click in the intro and begin as soon as possible. Alternatively, it's smoother to adapt the chord sequence so that you're in the new key before the song starts.

5. Always have a simple repeating sequence ready to allow flexibility for when the worship leader needs to jump back into the song or maybe if others need to give an exhortation, prayer, testimony, or the like.

Of course, the worship service has dimensions where it can be very spontaneous. You cannot always predict exactly how and when the transition will take place, but it's good to be as prepared as possible. It may be best to let just one minstrel (probably the keyboard player) take care of the transition and the others be ready to join at the start of the next song.

Being able to flow and function during transitional points in the worship service is very important. Having your worship material laid out and planned is very important as well. When there is a certain point in the praise and worship service where a transition needs to take place, you'll know how to navigate without it looking like you are lost. The emphasis here, of course, is not to limit your praise and worship experience to what you have mapped out and preplanned. You must be open to the Holy Spirit's moving.

The most important thing that you must remember is that praise and worship starts with you and God before you can start leading people anywhere. Blessings!

#worshipper4life

The Chamber Hall of Praise Library

"I will praise the LORD according to his righteousness: and will sing praise to the name of the LORD most high." Psalm 7:17

"The LORD is my strength and my shield; my heart trusted in him, and I am helped: therefore my heart greatly rejoiceth; and with my song will I praise him." Psalm 28:7

"Let them shout for joy, and be glad, that favour my righteous cause: yea, let them say continually, Let the LORD be magnified, which hath pleasure in the prosperity of his servant. And my tongue shall speak of thy righteousness and of thy praise all the day long." Psalm 35:27–28

"Know ye that the LORD he is God: it is he that hath made us, and not we ourselves; we are his people, and the sheep of his pasture. Enter into his gates with thanksgiving, and into his courts with praise: be thankful unto him, and bless his name. For the LORD is good; his mercy is everlasting; and his truth endureth to all generations." Psalm 100:3–5

"Sing, O daughter of Zion; shout, O Israel; be glad and rejoice with all the heart, O daughter of Jerusalem." Zephaniah 3:14

"Thou art my God, and I will praise thee: thou art my God, I will exalt thee. O give thanks unto the LORD; for he is good: for his mercy endureth forever." Psalm 118:28-29

"Rejoice in the Lord always: and again I say, Rejoice." Philippians 4:4

"Then I will go to the altar of God, to God my exceeding joy, yea upon the harp will I praise thee, O God my God." Psalm 43:4

"Praise the Lord! Sing to the Lord a new song, his praise in the assembly of the godly! Let Israel be glad in his Maker; let the children of Zion rejoice in their King! Let them praise his name with dancing, making melody to him with tambourine and lyre! For the Lord takes pleasure in his people; he adorns the humble with salvation. Let the godly exult in glory; let them sing for joy on their beds." Psalm 149:1–5 (ESV)

"Heal me, O LORD, and I shall be healed; save me, and I shall be saved, for thou art my praise." Jeremiah 17:14

"Through him then let us continually offer up a sacrifice of praise to God, that is, the fruit of lips that acknowledge his name." Hebrews 13:15 (ESV)

"I bless GOD every chance I get; my lungs expand with his praise. I live and breathe GOD; if things aren't going well, hear this and be happy: Join me in spreading the news; together let's get the word out. GOD met me more than halfway, he freed me from my anxious fears. Look at him; give him your warmest smile. Never hide your feelings from him. When I was desperate, I called out, and GOD got me out of a tight spot. GOD's angel sets up a circle of protection around us while we pray. Open your mouth and taste, open your eyes and see—how good God is. Blessed are you who run to him. Worship GOD if you want the best; worship opens doors to all his goodness." Psalm 34:1–9, The Message

Worship Chamber Quotes

"Worship is the sign that in giving myself completely to someone or something, I want to be mastered by it."

~ Harold Best ~

"I have discovered the password to the ATM of heaven. I pushed the button and healing fell out."

~ David Binion ~

"Reverential human acts of submission and homage before the divine Sovereign, in response to his gracious revelation of himself, and in accordance with his will."

~ Dan Block ~

"When I worship, I would rather my heart be without words than my words be without heart."

~ Lamar Boschman ~

"To worship God 'in spirit and in truth' is first and foremost a way of saying that we must worship God by means of Christ. In Him the reality has dawned and the shadows are being swept away (Hebrews 8:13). Christian worship is new covenant worship; it is gospel-inspired worship; it is Christ-centered worship; it is cross-focused worship."

~ D. A. Carson ~

"Worship is living our life individually and corporately as continuous living sacrifices to the glory of a person or thing."

~ Mark Driscoll ~

"Redemption is the means; worship is the goal. In one sense, worship is the whole point of everything. It is the purpose of history, the goal of the whole Christian story. Worship is not one segment of the Christian life among others. Worship is the entire Christian life, seen as a priestly offering to God. And when we meet together as a church, our time of worship is not merely a preliminary to something else; rather, it is the whole point of our existence as the body of Christ."

~ John Frame ~

"As heirs of Him who is King, we have His signet ring, which means we carry His face, we represent, which is to say to represent Jesus in the form of our worship."

~ Jenn Johnson ~

"Whenever His people gather and worship Him, God promises He will make His presence known in their midst. On the other hand, where God's people consistently neglect true spiritual worship, His manifest presence is rarely experienced."

~ Ralph Mahoney ~

"When we talk about praise and worship, some of the things that I've seen in many churches are that we often have a tendency to stay in praise and not move to the destination of worship. Our praise is the vehicle that leads us to worship. For some it's either lack of understanding or lack of maturity."

~ Dr. Judith McAllister ~

"Worship is not just an emotional experience. You must worship God in two ways: in spirit and in truth. In our congregations, we may have a lot of spirit but no truth. The truth only comes by the Word."

~ Pastor Donnie McClurkin ~

"Worship of the living and true God is essentially an engagement with him on the terms that he proposes and in the way that he alone makes possible."

~ David Peterson ~

"Strong affections for God, rooted in and shaped by the truth of Scripture—this is the bone and marrow of biblical worship."

~ John Piper ~

"Worship is everything we think, everything we say, and everything we do, revealing that which we treasure and value most in life."

~ Josh Riley ~

"Christians believe that true worship is the highest and noblest activity of which man, by the grace of God, is capable."

~ John Stott ~

"God is to be praised with the voice, and the heart should go therewith in holy exultation."

~ Charles H. Spurgeon ~

"Worship is the submission of all our nature to God. It is the quickening of conscience by His holiness; the nourishment of mind with His truth; the purifying of imagination by His Beauty; the opening of the heart to His love; the surrender of will to His purpose—and all of this gathered up in adoration, the most selfless emotion of which our nature is capable and therefore the chief remedy for that self-centeredness which is our original sin and the source of all actual sin."

~ William Temple ~

"To great sections of the church the art of worship has been lost entirely, and in its place has come that strange and foreign thing called the 'program.' This word has been borrowed from the stage and applied with sad wisdom to the type of public service which now passes for worship among us."

~ A. W. Tozer ~

"Worship is the believer's response to all they are—mind, emotions, will, body—to what God is and says and does."

~ Warren Wiersbe ~

"Worship is this inevitable result of the created catching a glimpse of the reality of the creator and then responding. Worship clearly identifies which kingdom you belong to. The person who knows the value and power of true worship will always find the ability to stand strong."

~ Darlene Zschech ~

About the Author

"Many call him the **Mail Man** because of his on point prophetic delivery of the Word of God; to others he's an anointed vessel with a 'right now' word for a prepared people..."

Dr. John D. Coleman was called by God at the age of 17 and was licensed and ordained at the age of 19 under the Pentecostal Assemblies of the World (P.A.W.). Dr. John has:

- an AA Degree in Business Management from Phillips College;
- a Bachelor of Arts in Ministry with an emphasis on Biblical Studies;
- a Master of Arts in Christian Education;
- and a Doctorate of Philosophy in Ministry from Midwest Christian College & Seminary.

Dr. John has a mandate to bring a realization to the body of Christ that it is God's desire for His people to establish a relationship with Him instead of a "religion-ship." He is playing a pivotal part in reaching this generation and equipping them to praise and worship God on a level that activates the gifts within them. A cloud of testimonies, including financial and healing miracles, have manifested as a result of his ministry.

In his first book *Power Points to Prosperous Living*, Dr. John elaborates on forty-one points that lead to prosperous living. He often emphasizes one of the points taken from this book:

"There are two types of people that come in your life: those that inspire you and those that expire you."

He has traveled and preached locally, nationally, and internationally, yet he is committed to his family and church, Kingdom Church Int'l., a non-denominational assembly in which he and his wife are both founders and pastors in the south suburbs of Chicago. Their vision for this local church is "to empower God's people for Kingdom living and Kingdom advancement in the earth."

Along with his wife, Kisia, Dr. John has spear-headed many community initiatives and outreach programs, raising tens of thousands of dollars to help families in need. Their effect and contributions in the communities that they service are too numerous to mention.

Dr. John and his wife live in a suburb of Chicago and are the proud parents of five children, two boys and three girls, which includes his two orphaned nieces and nephew.

Contact Information

Dr. John Coleman
Kingdom Church International
PO Box 596
Park Forest, Il 60466
708-872-8KCI
Email: pastorjdcoleman@sbcglobal.net

Twitter @Delandjcoleman
Facebook: www.facebook.com/deland.j.coleman